# FINDING
# FOCUS
## IN A BUSY WORLD

### HOW TO TUNE OUT THE NOISE
### AND WORK WELL UNDER PRESSURE

## JOSHUA SETH

To Suzy, Tiger, and Nikita
I've found my focus in life, and it is you.

# Table of Contents

# PART 3: Focus On Your Productivity .............79

# PART 4: Focus On Your Success ..................... 117

# Introduction

It's a common refrain: "I'm just so busy. I'm constantly being pulled in different directions and not getting anything done!" It can certainly be tough to focus on any one thing, to do it well and to completion, when there are so many demands on our attention all the time. It may seem like the only solution is to multitask and just work harder, but there is a far better way to find focus, work well under pressure, and actually enjoy the process.

In reality, we have no choice but to focus on one thing at a time. Multitasking is an illusion – it's simply the rapid shifting of focus. When we do that, when we continuously split our focus, it degrades the quality of our work. Things may get done, but they don't get done well.

People have become very busy in recent years, constantly on the run, endlessly scrolling through social media posts, texting while driving and talking, grabbing ready-made food and gobbling it down on the go, powering through the day with too little rest and too much distraction, doing a thousand things at once, focused on everything but the present moment. All that hyperconnected, always-on, busyness doesn't actually make them any more productive – it makes them more stressed out.

That trajectory leads to overwhelm and illness. It leads to

aggression and exhaustion. And that results in a lack of quality in your personal and professional life. At the end of the day, it leaves no time or room or energy for real human interactions. We're more connected than ever but we're also more isolated.

The pressure created by constant distractions can also take a toll on your health. It produces what psychologists call "background stress". The combination of distracted thinking and stressful living can destroy productivity, relationships, and your very quality of life. Without the proper tools and techniques to manage the daily onslaught of information and activities it can all become very overwhelming.

Believe me, as the father of two young children, I understand that completely. Both of my kids want nothing more than my complete focus and attention at all times. And I love to give that to them whenever possible. But I also need to focus on work each day, on staying healthy, and on all my other personal and professional relationships. Each area needs total focus, given to them in turn, in order to maintain balance and harmony.

As a corporate speaker and entertainer, continuously dealing with travel logistics, scheduling details, creative problem-solving, and the pressure of presenting in front of hundreds or even thousands of people on a regular basis, I've had to put systems in place that will allow me to continue producing quality results despite the fatigue that comes from being awoken every night by a baby and a toddler.

Although I've written this book for high-achieving adults at risk of becoming overwhelmed by work and information overload, I've kept my two children, Tiger and Nikita, in the back of my mind throughout the process. I thought, "If I could pass on to them everything really important and valuable that I've learned about playing on a high level without losing your sanity and sense of purpose, what would that be?" And the answer, it turns out, is this book.

My role as a husband and father is the most important part of my life. And what I'm sharing with you here is the best gift I can give my own family. It represents the distillation of a lifetime of learning and practical experience on how to focus your mind to minimize stress, maximize productivity, and achieve meaningful success.

I hope you'll approach this book with an open mind and a willingness to move past old habits, assumptions, and beliefs that may be holding you back from achieving all that you can in life.

Some of the ideas and exercises I'll share with you in this book may seem new, or unfamiliar, or even weird but if I've included them it's because they get results. I want to challenge you to shake things up a bit, look at things in a new way, and do things differently. You know what Einstein said: doing the same things repeatedly and expecting different results is the definition of insanity.

This book reveals techniques that I used to complete a 4 year University program in just 2 years (with a double major and honors level performance). I don't think I was smarter than anyone else – I was just very good at directing my focus and that produced amazing results.

Just imagine what you could accomplish if you could double your productivity while reducing the time needed to do it.

The same thing happened when I went to Hollywood as a voice over artist and was able to use these techniques to successfully navigate high pressure audition situations and land the starring role in the #1 cartoon on the air at that time.

A few years later, I began starring in TV specials around the world and once again the ability to stay calm, focused, and productive while being filmed in front of a live audience and broadcast to millions of people was invaluable.

In every instance, the ability to focus under pressure was what gave me the edge needed to succeed, and the results were life changing.

Just imagine what you can accomplish when fear, worry, anxiety, overwhelm, stress, and self-doubt are no longer a part of your life.

How much more energy you'll have when stress, diet, and exercise are all systemized and managed.

How much more effectively you'll work when you can focus on the process instead of the pressure.

When you have the right techniques and know how to use them, you can quickly clear your mind, find your focus, and diminish the distractions so you can become more happy, productive, and successful.

## Objectives

This book is about how to effectively focus on what's important and let go of everything that's not enjoyable, valuable, or productive.

There's so much to do these days that without calm, focused thoughts and actions there's almost no chance of keeping up with everything. But until you put the emotional, psychological, and physiological framework in place to support that approach, all the hard work and good intentions just lead to more unfinished business. Each of those areas needs to be addressed in order to achieve consistent, sustainable results.

The key to working well under pressure is relaxed concentration, the ability to focus on the task at hand until completion, and the clarity of mind to know what's worth doing in the first place.

In the service of those goals, I've divided this book into the following four parts:

*Part One – Focus On Your Thinking* provides exercises that can transform the underlying emotional and psychological conditions that have kept you feeling overworked and overwhelmed up until now.

*Part Two – Focus On Your Health* provides diet, exercise, and stress management solutions to the problem of living under constant pressure. If you lose your health, then it's difficult to focus on anything but regaining it. Here's how to stay healthy, minimize stress, and maximize energy.

*Part Three – Focus On Your Productivity* provides specific techniques you can use to start working with the kind of concentrated focus that will allow you to accomplish far more in less time and with higher quality.

*Part Four – Focus On Your Success* provides insights into the true meaning of success and explores several areas where you can direct your focus to acquire it.

Finding focus starts with quieting your mind and developing an awareness of the present moment. That is a skill which can be learned. In the next chapter we'll explore an easy way to practice that skill. It involves a discipline that some people find scary, others find relaxing, but ultimately is simply a very effective attention training technique. Can you guess what it is?

# Bonus & Backstory

Knowledge is not power. It's potential power. Knowledge in action is power. This book will give you the knowledge of what to do and your bonus audio recording will guide you through the process of actually doing it. Together they're a system which can help you become more focused, energized, and healthy.

So what is this bonus recording? A progressive relaxation meditation for stress reduction.

Now stay with me here! Just because I use words like "meditation" doesn't mean this will be a book about sitting on top of your desk in a lotus position and chanting Ohm.

My objective is to get you results and if that means exposing you to concepts that seem weird or unfamiliar, then so be it.

You don't have to believe in meditation to experience the benefits of it. It's simply taking a few moments each day to focus internally, breathe deeply, and relax.

Are you a Type A personality? I sure was. I carried a double course load all through college and completed it as fast as possible so I could get on with my life. Then I moved across the country to Hollywood and began the race to the top in the entertainment industry as a voice-over actor in TV and the movies. All through my twenties I was on the go, go, go. Life is short after all, and I didn't want to waste a minute of it. I never missed an opportunity to advance my career and was always "on call", as they say in the business.

Television is one of the most highly competitive fields in the world and I was determined to succeed at any cost. It took years but my single-minded focus paid off. Eventually I became one of the busiest voice-over actors in Hollywood, voicing the starring role in the #1 cartoon in the country at the time and doing hundreds of commercials, promos, animated movies, and TV. I even landed a role in *The Spongebob Squarepants Movie*. I should have been on top of the world. So why was I stressed out and aggravated all the time?

The insatiable drive for success had brought me money, a certain amount of fame, and every outward appearance of "success". The stress had helped ruin my first marriage and seriously degraded my health and happiness to the point where I burned out and left the business at the peak of my career. I spent the next six months on the beach in Santa Barbara reflecting, reassessing, and meditating on what success truly meant to me.

What I found was that I had been playing by the rules of somebody else's game and the proof was that the more I achieved in my career, the more dissatisfied I became. My climb to the top had instead become a race on a treadmill.

If success means reaching the top of the mountain ahead of your competitors, then I can tell you that all you find when you get there is that there's another, higher peak ahead of you.

Every time you think you've reached the top, another vista reveals itself. That's because there is no top. There is only the climb. Or to put it another way: there is no destination, there is only the process. And I hadn't been enjoying the process because I thought of it as something to get through on the way to a destination that didn't even exist.

What I didn't fully comprehend at the time is that the process is the reward. The work itself is the success I'd been striving for. The reason it didn't feel rewarding was because I was focused on the goal not the process. I was working myself to the point of exhaustion, never taking the time to rest, recharge, reflect, or refocus. Never appreciating the present moment. Always looking ahead to the next step on the climb to stay ahead of the competition.

What I eventually discovered is that when you're focused on the process of working in the present moment then the work itself becomes it's own reward. You'll find that innovation is more fulfilling than competition and the only worthy competitor is the ideal of your own best self. Taking each step to move into alignment with that ideal is a journey worth taking and it has nothing to do with any outward appearance of success.

That path moved me in an entirely different direction in life, full of exciting adventures as a corporate speaker and entertainer that have literally taken me around the world. You never really know what you're capable of achieving until you decide to live life on your own terms. Once you start to define success according to what it means to you personally, the results become far more gratifying and endlessly exciting.

To find that path which is uniquely yours requires silencing the noise of daily distractions enough to hear your own inner voice. Finding a balance between movement and stillness, busyness and rest, sound and silence. That's where the music is. Music exists because of the silence between the notes, without which there would be only noise.

Focusing internally, meditating, and doing the exercises in this book are the keys to bridging the gap between working yourself to exhaustion and making productive, sustainable, satisfying progress in life.

Meditation has proven to be a safe and effective method of natural stress reduction and is used by high achievers in every field throughout the world. Daily meditation with systematic relaxation will keep you motivated, energized, and consciously aware of the stress in your body and mind so you can relax, let it melt away, and move through the world with a calm awareness of self that communicates personal power.

You'll begin to develop a more calm, focused mindset as you systemize this process. Soon, without thinking about it, you will find it easier to handle the pressures that come with higher levels of productivity and responsibility. You'll enjoy the journey much more too, in harmony with the present moment, energized, and connected to yourself.

## What is Meditation?

Meditation is the process of focusing awareness, internally on yourself in the present moment, and being at one with the breath. It's also important to use that time to feel gratitude for what you have and the people in your life.

That's easier to accomplish at first with a skilled guide, such as myself, which is why I've provided you with that bonus audio recording on the website.

It's a free, effective, natural way to reduce your stress and focus on becoming the person you want to be. It's as important for your mind as exercise is for your body.

How do you practice meditation? Simply find a comfortable spot where you can safely assume a relaxed pose, seated or lying down, and close your eyes. Turn your focus inward, breathe deeply, and relax into an awareness of yourself in the present moment.

It can help to focus on the whispered "Ahhhh" sound, called Ujjiya breathing, described in Chapter 3. Calming your mind and focusing on an awareness of the breath in the present moment is the objective. Adding gratitude is the next step once you become comfortable with that basic technique.

After a while you'll be able to find other opportunities to make meditation a part of your daily routine. You won't even need to close your eyes to achieve results. I meditate every morning in the shower.

For years now I've played the same song and showered in the same sequence so as to create a ritual out of the routine and remove my conscious mind from the process. I breathe slowly and deeply and focus on all that I have to be grateful for in life. When the song is over I conclude the shower and step into my day – refreshed, relaxed, and energized.

That's meditation every bit as much as sitting with your eyes closed and legs crossed while chanting Ohm. Do it in a way that makes sense for you. It's just a tool to help you achieve focused relaxation. One of many.

You can use the audio program on the website to guide you through a progressive relaxation meditation with calming background music.

I think you'll be pleasantly surprised by the results. Many people tell me they feel so relaxed afterwards, it's as though they just had a massage. A massage for your mind :-)

You can get started right now by downloading your free guided meditation for stress reduction at www.findingfocusbook.com/meditation

# PART 1

## FOCUS ON YOUR THINKING

# 1

# Thoughts on Thinking

*"Enthusiasm releases the drive to carry you over obstacles
and adds significance to all that you do"*
**– Norman Vincent Peale**

et excited! Really. You are about to discover how to focus
G your mind in ways that have taken me years to discover and
can literally change the very quality of your life. By the end of
this section you will know how to tap into the power of your
subconscious mind to achieve more by doing less so that you can
become more productive, effective, and successful.

The premise is simple: your mind and body are connected so
by changing your mind, you can change your life. I'm not talking
about changing your opinions or beliefs (except possibly about
yourself). I'm talking about changing the thinking that influences
your habits and behaviors – because our habits, behaviors, and
expectations shape the course of our lives and directly impact our
level of productivity and success.

Your thoughts and beliefs will ultimately shape your physical
reality. Neurons that fire together, wire together. Your thoughts
and feelings over time physically weave together the very fabric of
your brain.

You can apply a few simple strategies to change your internal
perspective, the ideas and images going through your head,
and get dramatic results. And just like I do when speaking to
organizations, I've presented these concepts as actionable exercises.

Activities you can do today to achieve immediate results.

Here's an example: When you first wake up in the morning, do you reach for your phone and check your news feed? Is that news full of things that disturb you emotionally? Did you know that during those first 20 minutes of consciousness each morning you're in a natural Theta brain wave state that mimics the level of suggestibility people commonly refer to as hypnosis?

So what does all that mean? It means that the messages you put into your brain upon first awaking can influence your emotions and outlook for the rest of the day. If you simply wait 20-30 minutes to reach for that smart phone or turn on the news, and instead follow the suggestions in Chapter 15, you can better cope with all the little emotional upsets and agitations that occur throughout the day. By changing that one little habit of mind you can change the course of your entire day.

Here's an interesting exercise: How long can you go without looking at social media or the news? 20 minutes? 30 minutes? An hour? All day? How do you feel as a result? Less stressed out? More positive and happy? Or jonesing like an addict in need of a fix? Believe me, it's an experiment worth doing and could even save your relationship, as we'll discuss in a bit. Here's another one…

How about your health? There is no success without wellness. Productivity suffers when physical fitness is ignored. That's why I've devoted Chapter 11 to a ten point eating plan and one simple activity you can do that will fill you with energy and good health. And if you're like most people, you'll even drop a few pounds in the process.

And let's not forget, the number one culprit of lost productivity, illness, and fatigue in our society. Stress. An astounding 75-90% of doctor visits are caused by stress-related symptoms. The Occupational Safety and Health Administration (OSHA) has even declared stress a hazard of the workplace. Stress costs American industry more than $300 billion annually.

That's $300 Billion with a B. Or to put it another way, $7,500 per employee spent annually in the U.S. on stress-related compensation claims, reduced productivity, unanticipated absenteeism, health insurance costs, medical expenses, and employee turnover due to largely preventable causes.

Stress is at the heart of so many problems that if people were to make just one change that could impact everything else – from physical health, to emotional well-being, to productivity, to relationships – that change would be to manage stress better.

There's a creeping quality to stress. A pressure that builds up over time until what feels normal is anything but. If you hook a person up to a TENS machine, which delivers a series of electric pulses to stimulate the nervous system, the initial setting has to be on the lower end of the range. The body would recoil if too intense a shock is delivered at the starting point. But the severity of the shocks can be significantly ratcheted up over the course of just a few minutes as the body acclimates to the new level of stimulus. What would have been shockingly unacceptable at the start of the session is barely felt by the end of it.

This is what happens when you live under constant pressure. You may not even be aware of the effect it's having on every area of your life because over time it begins to feel normal. That doesn't make it any less debilitating. Just less likely to be addressed. This becomes what psychologists call "background stress" and continues to weigh heavy in the heart, mind, and body until a moment of crises occurs, like the loss of a job or a marriage or one's health. Then the effects of unmanaged stress become all too clear, all too fast.

On a day to day basis, the cumulative effects of stress can manifest in a variety of ways: headaches, constant fatigue, a lack of humor, emotional fragility, poor digestion, an inability to focus or to sleep, disorientation, anger or depression – the list goes on and on. And although the symptoms are quite real and can become quite serious, the underlying root cause of stress can be dealt with very efficiently with the ideas, exercises, and challenges laid out in this book.

Once implemented, the gradual dissipation of background stress is the very thing that can create an awareness of how much stress was there in the first place. It's only when you begin to focus on productive actions in the present moment that you realize how much stress was weighing you down and holding you back all along.

Focusing on productive action in the present moment is the key to working well under pressure. Just as the golfer must focus solely on the mechanics of his swing and not get distracted by the emotional charge from the previous swing, or the path the ball ultimately takes once hit, so too you must train your brain to focus on the process of your actions in the present moment with emotional detachment from the outcome. Being able to do that consistently is a total game changer in business and in life.

I'd like to show you some easy to master techniques that will reduce your stress, increase your focus, and improve your productivity throughout the day. Because the truth is that it's within your power right now, today, to completely change the way you react to working under pressure and manage your responses in a way that puts you back in control of your life.

A bold claim? You bet it is. But what if I'm right?

The minimal effort it will take you to learn and apply the strategies I've outlined for you in this book can have an enormous impact on your level of personal productivity and professional success.

You may be tempted to jump ahead to the sections that interest you, such as the 21 Productivity Tips in Part 3, but there is such a thing as context and if you skip around you'll risk losing that all important component. We're building a foundation here and, as you know, a strong foundation leads to a lasting structure.

# 2

# Creating Confidence

*"Always remember you are braver than you believe,*
*stronger than you seem, and smarter than you think."*
**– Christopher Robin**, *The Many Adventures*
*of Winnie the Pooh*

M y father is a psychologist and hypnotherapist, so I grew up understanding how to tap into the power of your subconscious mind to change your habits, manage your emotions, and increase your confidence. Basically, how to focus your awareness to maximize effectiveness. It always seemed to be a very straightforward proposition to me. Not so for most people. These concepts simply aren't taught in our culture.

Now that I speak to organizations about how to find focus and work well under pressure, I continually find that these time-tested, proven techniques are new and unfamiliar to my audiences.

People are very often surprised to discover that they can make a few small changes in their mindset and perspective and create an internal state conducive to greater focus and productivity. It's easy and I'm excited to show you how.

Your mind is the most amazing computer in the world and you are the programmer that runs it. These programs influence your thoughts, emotions, and behaviors and they reside in your subconscious mind. The exercises in this book are like upgrading the software and rebooting your internal computer.

Subconscious reprogramming has been used for years by countless athletes, celebrities, and high achievers to find focus, increase performance, and maintain a centered attitude of calm and well-being. But for the vast majority of people, the benefits of this "brain retraining" remain completely unknown. They think these people are simply super-human when in reality they are people, just like you and me, who have tapped into something inside themselves that allows them to see their goals as closer, bigger, and easier to reach than their competitors.

What's your goal? To manage stress better? To feel more rested? To finally get in shape? To have more energy? To be more confident? To be able to handle more responsibility? To become more productive? To have more meaningful relationships? To lead a happier, healthier life? To achieve a more fulfilling level of success?

I'm excited to show you how to tap into the power of your subconscious mind to achieve these goals faster and more easily than you ever thought possible.

This is more than a book. It's an owner's manual for your mind.

## Anchoring Exercise

Confidence is the key to self improvement. Believing you can overcome any obstacle and succeed no matter what. So let's create a Confidence Anchor to give you a feeling of personal power that you can summon at will as we move though the *Finding Focus* process.

Just as the anchor of a boat steadies it in stormy seas, so too can this associative conditioning exercise be used to steady yourself amidst the changing tides of life and living.

1.  Remember a time when you felt confident. Cool, calm, and collected. See what you saw at that time, hear what you heard, and feel what it felt like to have that level of personal power and command of the situation. (If you can't remember a specific time that fits that description, then imagine what it would be like to feel that way now).

2.  Replay that experience over and over in your mind, each time making the colors brighter, the sounds bigger, the feelings stronger.

3.  When you've made that picture strong and vivid in your mind, squeeze the thumb and middle finger of your dominant hand together. That will anchor the feeling of confidence to the physical sensation of the pressure between your thumb and middle finger.

4.  Now think about a situation from your past where you felt a lack of confidence. Squeeze your thumb and middle finger together and feel a wave of confidence spread throughout your body. Imagine feeling that confident in the previous situation.

5.  Still pressing your thumb and middle finger together, remember any stressful elements from that situation and imagine yourself now overcoming any and all obstacles with cool, calm, confidence. You are bigger and more resourceful while any problematic people and situations are smaller and less significant. You move confidently, seeing others as though they were moving in slow motion, knowing all the answers, easily overcoming anything in your way. Feel how good that feels.

6.  Think about that memory now. Do you feel less stressed out and more confident? Repeat steps 4 and 5 until you do.

7.  Think about a person or situation that is currently causing you stress in your life. Press your thumb and middle finger together and feel a wave of confidence spread throughout your body. Imagine feeling that confident when interacting with that person or while in that situation.

8.  Still pressing your thumb and middle finger together, imagine yourself doing everything perfectly in that situation. Saying just the right thing at just the right time to diffuse any stress or tension, seeing others as though they were moving in slow motion, knowing all the answers, easily overcoming anything in your way. Feeling how good that feels.

9.  Think about that person or situation now. Do you feel less stressed out and more confident? Repeat steps 7 and 8 until you do.

10. Apply the preceding process to any disempowering memories and any currently active situations and relationships in your life until the thought of them makes you feel less stressed out and more confident and in control.

Now that you have this Confidence Anchor you can use it whenever you need to trigger self-confidence in any situation. It's a Pavlovian response that gets stronger with repetition. Each time you go through this process, it will become easier to reduce stress and increase confidence.

The anchor becomes stronger every time you use it because your mind cannot tell the difference between real experiences and those that are vividly imagined. These visualizations will become your new reality over time and your behaviors will emanate from that new, more confident perspective. This is called *subconscious reprogramming* and we'll be doing a lot of it throughout this book. It's a safe, fast, effective way to tune out the noise, find focus, and alleviate pressure.

# 3

# Breathing Better

*"If you want to conquer the anxiety of life,
live in the moment, live in the breath" –* **Amit Ray**

**"**Take a nice deep breath. Now release and relax." I've opened every single one of my presentations with those words for over a decade because they put the audience in a state of focused relaxation and allow us all to achieve amazing results during the rest of our time together.

At my live events, I demonstrate human potential through the power of the mind to affect our physical realities. I do this using a combination of psychological principles, Neuro-Linguistic Programming (NLP), and, and the techniques presented in this book. These demonstrations of "mind power" have literally taken me around the world, performing for hundreds of the largest and most well-respected universities and corporations in existence over the past decade. The response has been amazing. These short presentations have had long lasting effects and been some of the most gratifying, fulfilling work I've done throughout my career.

Just seeing the light turn on in someone's eyes when they do one of these exercises and realize, maybe for the first time, that they can actually achieve more with less effort – in a way, just by thinking about it – is truly awe-inspiring.

Let's do one of these exercises right now. It's a breathing technique called Ujjayi.

Why focus on the breath? Because your mind is like a kite and your breath is the string that can direct it. Without guidance, your mind will float this way and that, naturally drifting with the changing winds of the moment, seemingly out of your control.

As you learn to guide your mind's focus, you will gain the power to control its direction and fly where you want to go, not where external events and other people's realities take you.

This process starts with the breath.

When you breathe slowly and deeply, consciously focusing your awareness on the action of the breath itself, it has a calming and energizing effect. It's the beginning of the meditative process and you can do it anytime, anywhere, with your eyes open or closed. This process will give you a feeling of control that can help make you more decisive and effective in stressful situations.

Think about it: how do you breathe when you're panicked? Slow, sharp breaths. How do you breathe when you're crying? Slow, sharp breaths. How do you breathe when you're "in the zone"? Slow, deep, and focused. You can snap yourself out of feeling stressed and into feeling empowered through breath, thought, movement, and posture. We'll address each of those areas through this book. For now though, let's just start with the breath.

## Ujjayi (pronounced oo-jai) Breath

This is an ancient breathing technique to calm the mind and body. When translated into the English, it literally means "to become victorious" or "to gain mastery."

The benefits of mindfully practicing this form of breathing, for even a few minutes a day, are many:

1. Releases physical and mental tension
2. Improves concentration
3. Increases capacity for focus
4. Creates an awareness of self

5.  Minimizes external distractions
6.  Instills an empowering sense of calm alertness
7.  Changes your emotional state so you can reengage from a more centered perspective

It's very simple to do and the more you practice it, the easier it will be for you to maintain over sustained periods of time.

## Breathing Exercise

Sit still for a moment. It doesn't matter what's going on around you. You are going to focus your attention on the present moment and specifically the action of your mindful breathing.

Slightly constrict the back of your throat so that as you release your breath it makes a whispered "ahhhhh" sound, as if you're fogging a pair of sunglasses. It should sound like the soothing sound of the ocean.

Breathe in through your nose while opening your throat to allow a similar (although different sounding) "ahhh" on the inhalation.

Now continue breathing slowly and deeply, in through your nose and out through your mouth. Always making that whispered "ahhhhh" sound on both the inhalation and the exhalation. Never pushing it, just letting it flow.

Be aware of the breath and the process of breathing itself. Focus on that action in the present moment. Don't count the breath or the time you spend doing this process. Just immerse yourself in the experience and emerge when you feel ready.

Once you are comfortable with this process it can become a valuable tool for tuning out the noise, alleviating stress, and overcoming overwhelm. No one even needs to know you're doing it. You will become more calm, centered, proactive, and focused as a result.

# 4

# Letting Go of the Past

*"When I let go of what I am, I become what I might be"*
— Lao Tzu

As we begin to Focus on the present it's helpful to let go of any past experiences that may have been holding you back. Everyone has had traumas and unpleasant memories occur at some point. That's just a part of life. But how we chose to deal with them and when or if we ever move past them can be a determining factor in whether we ever get over them.

Dr. Richard Bandler (co-creator of NLP) developed a technique to disassociate the emotional charge from undesirable memories. It's a fast, effective way to close the door on that part of your past you wish to leave behind so that you can fully and freely step into your future.

The exercise below is my modified version of that original technique. I've added a few extra steps that expand its functionality so you can use it to desensitize fears and phobias as well.

Disclaimer: if you're suffering from a serious trauma, phobia, or disorder, please seek professional help. Otherwise, pick something you'd like to get over and let's make that happen now.

# Dissociation Exercise

1. Imagine you're sitting in a movie theater and you're beginning to drift off. Half asleep but still watching the images on the screen.

2. See yourself float up and out of your body into the projection booth in the back of the theater. You can still see the images on the screen from way back there and you can also see yourself, sitting down below, looking up at the movie.

3. The movie is of an unpleasant memory from your past. It starts just before the event occurred and ends just after the successful completion on the other side of the situation.

4. See a still image of that "moment before" up on the screen. From the safety of the projection booth, far back from the event itself and behind a wall of solid glass, watch yourself way down in the theater watching the film of what happened up on the screen. Continue watching yourself watch the movie until the moment after your successful completion on the other side of the event. Now freeze that "moment after" picture up on the screen.

5. Now watch as the film begins running backwards at high speed. Everything that happened is sped up and running in reverse, even the sound, until the moment before anything ever happened in the first place. It's comical.

6. Repeat steps 4 and 5 several times.

7. Now run steps 4 and 5 forward and backward with all the color drained out of the picture. Repeat this 3 times.

8. Now run steps 4 and 5 with all the color drained out of the picture and everyone in the movie dressed as funny clowns. Funny clown hair, clown shoes, clown noses, and silly music. Repeat this 3 times.

9. Repeat steps 4 through 8 until all the emotional charge is drained from the memory.

10. Now float back down into your body in the theater, get up, walk out into the light of day, and move on with your life.

# 5

# Guided Visualization

*"Create a vision of who you want to be, and then live
into that picture as if it were already true"*
**– Arnold Schwarzenegger**

Let's move on to a guided visualization exercise. If you've never experienced this process it's a very powerful technique to get your mind, body, and emotions to focus on what's possible rather than what is not. It focuses your mind on possibilities rather than problems.

If it's safe for you to do so now, put your feet flat on the floor, hands in your lap so they're not touching, roll your shoulders back, and just relax. Just relax and go with it. Now take a nice deep breath in. And then slowly release and relax. That's right. Nice and slow.

Now take another deep breath in. And as you release this breath let go of any stress, tension, fear, and negativity. Just breathe it out and let it go.

Now take the deepest breath of all… and hold it. 1, 2, 3, 4, 5. Now just let *everything* go, release, and relax completely.

Keep breathing deeply, imagining the sound of my voice. Noticing how good it feels… just to relax, just to do something good for yourself today.

Now imagine if you will that you are in a safe place.

Whatever a safe place means to you, imagine you are there now in your mind. Visualize what it looks like to be in that safe place…

in your mind. See what it looks like. Hear the sounds that are present in that place of safety and security. Most importantly, feel what it feels like to be in that safe place in your mind right now.

Now imagine you are there in that safe place with a person you respect and admire. See what that person you respect and admire looks like. Hear what it sounds like to be in their presence now. Feel what it feels like to be with that person you respect and admire. Here in that place of safety and security.

You are safe. You are complete. You are peaceful and perfect.

Now holding onto those feelings of peace and tranquility, safety and security, respect and admiration. Take a deep breath in, and exhale the word HAH! Push that sound out from your abdomen – HAH! Now breathe 5 short breaths in and out rapidly while making the HAH! sound on your exhalation. Now breathe slowly and deeply again as you roll your head, shoulders, and body into an open posture that feels comfortable and content to you.

How do you feel?

A bit more relaxed? More calm and alert? That's simply because you're breathing deeply and focusing internally on yourself.

This guided visualization is an example of Neuro-Linguistic Programming, better known as NLP. These are very powerful waking hypnosis techniques and, in this case, it helps you to lock in and engage to create the conditions for calm, focused learning.

If you enjoyed the experience, reread the preceding section and do the entire process again. I used that technique myself when I was in college to focus in class and prime myself for learning. It worked so well I completed a four year program in two years with a double major and no coffee. I was simply more calm, focused, alert, and receptive to learning then most people around me and it accelerated my progress almost without my knowing it.

Brain retraining exercises like this can help you to tap into the power of your subconscious mind and allow you to make all kinds of positive changes in your life.

# 6

# Reframe Your Self-Talk

*"Love yourself first and everything else falls into line.*
*You really have to love yourself to get anything done in this world"*
**– Lucille Ball**

Let's focus now on your internal dialogue and retrain your brain to talk positively about yourself. This is called "reframing your self-talk".

Self-talk refers to the messages that you give yourself when you talk to yourself in your own mind. This is a very powerful technique, the effects of which will resonate throughout every area of your life.

*The Mirror Exercise* is an easy and effective way to get yourself in the habit of saying positive things about yourself while in a peaked emotional state. Emotional engagement is the key to realizing the potential of this exercise. Just saying the words is not enough – you need to really mean them.

So what is *The Mirror Exercise?*

The first twenty minutes of the day and the last twenty minutes of the day, you're in a naturally hypnotic state. You're in Theta brain wave state. Throughout the rest of the day you cycle through Beta, Alpha, Theta, or Delta brainwave states.

Delta is what you experience in deep sleep. Beta is where you are for most of the day, working and interacting with people. Alpha is when you're zoning out, reading a book, or driving your car. But when you're in Theta state, that's when you're most susceptible to suggestion and in a naturally hypnotic frame of mind, like when having a lucid dream. You dream that you're falling and your body lurches, even though you're lying flat in your bed. Have you ever experienced that? That's Theta brain wave state.

You're driving somewhere you've been many times, like your own home, but you miss your exit. You weren't aware of the exit. You weren't in your conscious mindset or you would have seen your exit. But you weren't unconscious either. If you were unconscious you would have driven off the road or into another car. You simply passed your exit without noticing your surroundings. You were driving the car subconsciously, on autopilot, and your mind was a million miles away.

That's what it's like to experience Theta brain wave state. You're in that state first thing in the morning and last thing at night. When you're in Theta state, it's very productive to focus on your own improvement. Focus on becoming the person you want to be. The messages will get in and take hold much more easily than at other times of the day.

Unfortunately, most people waste this opportunity by focusing on the news and social media during these highly suggestible moments – focusing on what other people are doing, other people's problems, things they can't control or change anyway.

Those first and last 20-30 minutes of the day are golden moments that can be harnessed to move you closer to fulfilling your own potential. Instead of focusing on the world around you, turn your focus inward and do *The Mirror Exercise* to make the most of those naturally hypnotic opportunities.

## The Mirror Exercise

Take a picture of yourself when you were at your peak level of fitness, when you felt great, and you were happy. Take a picture of that and stick it on the mirror. Look at that picture and look yourself in the eye.

Look at the picture, look at yourself, look at the picture, look at yourself and with deep feeling and emotion say, "I love myself". In fact, say that right now. "I love myself." Go ahead and do it out loud, and really mean it. "I love myself."

If you're reading this at the office, I'll bet you got some strange looks!

I know it sounds cheesy, believe me I know, but it works. If you can't do that – if you can't say, "I love myself" – then you may as well put this book down or give it to someone who will, because I can't help you if you won't help yourself.

All this subconscious reprogramming won't do anything for you if you can't first say that you love yourself and that you are deserving of a better life and a better quality of life experience.

These are very powerful words – "I love you" – and even more powerful when you say them to yourself, because the more you love yourself the more self-esteem you will generate. The more self-love you have, the more you have to give to your family, to your friends, to your co-workers and society at large. And because you're resonating on that higher level, people who are also resonating on that level will recognize it in you, respond to it, and better quality life experiences will come your way.

If you want people to start treating you better, you have to start treating yourself better first.

Do *The Mirror Exercise* first thing in the morning and last thing at night for three weeks straight and you'll start to see amazing changes in your life. It will rewire your brain and change the self-talk messages you give yourself throughout the day. You'll literally be hypnotizing yourself into believing that you are deserving of a better life and the effects of this change in mindset and attitude can elevate everything you do.

The *Mirror Exercise* only takes a minute to do but can energize your whole day. Are you going to start doing it?

Commit to putting that picture up on your mirror today. Then do it, with full emotional commitment, each and every day. Every morning and every night. You will start to feel a personal power and sense of well-being that will grow with each passing day. In a month it will become second nature. People will notice the difference. You'll notice the difference. Just do it! Start today.

# 7

# Erase Worry
# & Fear

*"Worry is interest paid on trouble before it comes due"*
– **William Ralph Inge**

Focus on what you can control and let go of what you can't. Worry and fear are stress producing and distractions. Left unmanaged that stress can progress to anxiety and ultimately even panic attacks. An extreme (but not uncommon) example would be when a person who has a fear of loud noises stops going to crowded places in order to avoid the possibility of encountering them and ultimately ends up cloistered in their own home as an agoraphobic. This is how a simple fear or phobia can become generalized over time and end up diminishing your entire life experience. It can happen to anyone.

Less dramatically, the common fear of public speaking keeps many would-be leaders from ever magnifying their own voice and realizing their true potential. The fear of public speaking is often said to be more common in our society than the fear of death. That's not logical of course, but emotions aren't governed by logic.

Irrational worries and fears are examples of our mind's ability to spin out of control and limit our ability to perform at our peak potential. So why do people do it? To feel safe.

Does it make you any safer to worry about something, anything? Of course not.

Worry does you no good whatsoever. It's a purposeless activity that focuses on worst-case scenarios without ever considering solutions. It's ruminative and unproductive.

I can hear the resistance to that statement now. "But what if I'm worrying about something important, like my children's safety?"

Then instead of worrying, do something to make them safer. Think of an action you can take that will create a benefit instead of an apprehension. Then do that thing that will create the safety you desire to the degree that you can create it.

Ultimately, we all have to come to terms with the fact that life is fleeting and there is only so much we can do to protect it. Do what you can and then let go of what you can't.

Easier said than done, right? Well, I'm about to share with you a form of "psychological acupressure" designed to dissolve worry and fear. It's easy to learn, doesn't cost anything, and can achieve remarkable results in only a few minutes. It's commonly known as EFT.

The Emotional Freedom Technique (EFT) was developed by Gary Craig in the 1990s and has gained a worldwide following of enthusiastic practitioners. When I first heard about it, my BS meter went into high alert. It's typically described as "tapping on energy meridians". Energy meridians? That's a bit new-agey for me.

Where's the proof that "energy meridians" even exist? And the technique just seemed so easy to implement compared to the reported results that I was more than a bit skeptical. But one of the benefits of having been alive nearly half a century now is that I've learned not to be too quick to judge things that may seem new or unfamiliar.

I used it for the first time on a woman whose fear of birds was keeping her from getting off of the cruise ship we were on (lest she be attacked by pigeons or something). The results were stunning. Twenty minutes later and her decades-old fear was literally erased from her mind. Sapped of it's power. And she was happily walking along the open deck and looking forward to her day in port.

Next, a woman who'd observed this transformation asked if I'd address her fear of elevators. I showed her how to do the basic EFT sequence and guess what? Twenty minutes later we were riding up and down in the elevator!

I had my proof. These weren't unsubstantiated anecdotes. After all, I saw these changes occurring in real time with my own eyes and I've been privileged to facilitate similar transformations countess times in the years since then.

In the face of these realities, my skepticism disappeared. In it's place began to grow a profound respect for the brilliant simplicity of the Emotional Freedom Technique.

So what is EFT? Think of it as a non-invasive alternative to acupuncture that simultaneously addresses the psychological and emotional root causes of worry and fear. It's similar to acupressure but is self-administered and incorporates positive affirmations that have the potential to desensitize the emotional charge from past experiences or future concerns.

There have been a lot of variations and "improvements" on EFT over the years, but I'm not convinced they offer any additional benefits over the basic technique. So the basic technique is what I'll describe here.

But first, what are the pros and cons of using EFT?

Pros:

- It's safe and pain-free (no drugs or negative side effects)
- No needles (it's non-invasive)
- No medications
- It's free (you can do this to yourself)
- It's easy to learn and implement
- It's effective on a wide variety of irrational worries and fears

Cons:

It might not work.

That's a pretty big con but look at it this way: it's possible that you go through this process and don't see the results you wanted to achieve. If so, so what? It didn't cost you anything, only took a few minutes to do, and you're no worse for having opened yourself up to the possibility that it may indeed work.

So the only "con" is really just an acknowledgement that it's not a panacea, magic-bullet, or cure-all. If you need professional help with something, then by all means go get it.

If, on the other hand, you're simply holding yourself back in life because of some irrational worry or fear, then what are you waiting for? Let's get tapping!

## The Basic EFT Sequence

First, get in a safe, quiet place, free of distractions and the curious eyes of others. This can look a bit weird the first time you do it and there's no need to put yourself in a situation where you might feel self-conscious.

Next, remove your glasses, watches, bracelets, basically anything that would interfere with tapping on the following areas:

1. The top of your head
2. The middle of your eyebrows
3. The bone at the base of each eye
4. The area between your nose and upper lip
5. The chin area below your bottom lip
6. The collar bone
7. The area under the arm and about 4" below your arm pit

# The EFT Application

1. Determine the specific worry or fear you want to address

2. Rate it's severity on a scale of 0-10 (with 0 being nonexistent and 10 being extremely severe)

3. Create a Set-Up Phrase. This is a statement of the problem that you want to solve and an affirmation that you still love and accept yourself no matter what.

   Example of a Set-Up Phrase: Even though I (state the problem), I completely love, accept, and forgive myself.

4. Say your set-up phrase while tapping your Karate Chop point 7-10 times. This is the soft area of your hand, below the base of your pinky finger.

5. Create a Reminder Phrase. This phrase reminds you of your set-up phrase and is spoken aloud while tapping on a sequence of acupressure points. Simply repeat the name of the issue you are addressing as you tap the points.

6. Tap the 7 areas of your body listed above while saying your Reminder Phrase out loud. 7-10 taps on each spot before moving on to the next area. Tap using the tips of 2 or 4 fingers (whichever is more comfortable for you). If you have long finger nails, then use the pads of your fingers instead of the tips. This isn't magic. Tap in a way that is comfortable for you and gets results.

7. After you've completed the preceding sequence, rate the severity of your worry or fear on the 0-10 scale you used earlier.

8. Repeat steps 6 and 7 until you determine that the severity of your worry or fear has diminished to a 2 or lower.

9. On the last round of tapping, change your spoken phrase to acknowledge the results you've obtained. Make sure it's in the present tense.

   **Example:** I'm free of (state your previous problem). Or (state your previous problem) is gone from my life now.

10. If your previous irrational worry or fear relates to an activity that is now safe for you to do, then go out and do it immediately. Prove to yourself that you are in control of your own mind – it doesn't control you.

If you were afraid of enclosed spaces, then go stand in an enclosed space for a few minutes and breathe through the wonderful new experience you've allowed yourself to have.

If you were afraid of public speaking, then raise your voice, loud and proud, and announce something to the world. It can be anything really. Just do it. The worst that will happen is people look at you funny for a moment and then go about their business.

No one will care except you. For you, it will be the first of many victories that can unleash your potential to move mountains. That's the power of EFT to erase worry and fear.

# PART 2

## FOCUS ON YOUR HEALTH

# 8

# Motivating vs Debilitating Stress

*"Stress should be a powerful driving force, not an obstacle"*
**– Bill Phillips**

Some stress *can* be good. Yeah, I said it. There's a kind of stress that's actually motivating and keeps pushing you forward. It lights a fire under you. There's a name for that kind of stress. It's called Eustress.

Occasionally people can be resistant to implementing stress reduction strategies because they think it will cause them to lose their edge. That stress is actually driving them to get more done in less time. But they're actually confusing Eustress with Distress.

Eustress is the motivating stress that gives you an edge. It lights a fire under you that's manageable enough to leap over. Like a deadline or a competition. It gives you an opportunity to rise to the challenge and find out what you're capable of achieving.

Distress is when that fire gets out of control and threatens to burn your house down – when your only concern is to either fight the flames or run for your life!

Constructive versus destructive stress is like blowing air into a balloon. A little bit makes it functional – a lot can cause it to pop. The air went from being a constructive force (eustress) to a destructive force (distress) in an instant. Same air. Different outcome.

So when we're talking about stress reduction, we're not really talking about the kind that can motivate you, the productive kind. We're actually talking about the kind of stress that causes people to shut down, feel overwhelmed, bury their head in their hands, and ultimately get sick.

When you eliminate that kind of stress, you will actually become more focused, have more energy, and develop more of an edge than you had before. You can still get feelings of overwhelm and fatigue from time to time, but your ability to cope with them will be much better and the effects will not be as severe or last as long.

The skills you'll learn throughout this book will help you to respond proactively when those feelings do arise so you can get back on track and get on with your life.

## So What is Stress?

Stress is an automatic, physiological response in the body and mind to a disturbance in equilibrium. This is characterized by the release of the hormones cortisol and adrenaline in the bloodstream, the onset of negative emotions, and the impulse to act aggressively or run away from the problem (fight or flight).

But more importantly, what is it that causes the stress response to activate in the first place? That's the part we can actually do something about.

Stress is simply caused by a threat, real or imagined, to our sense of balance and order in life. Ultimately, it's something that we want to change but are powerless to do anything about.

The symptoms of stress tend to manifest externally as interpersonal conflict and poor productivity – and internally as anger, depression, fatigue, and anxiety.

Chronic stress can create a feeling of overwhelm, like you just can't keep up. Tying to keep on top of things but never getting ahead. Going in too many directions at once. Unable to focus. Anxious and agitated.

The results of unmanaged stress can be devastating to your work, your health, your relationships, and the very quality of your life.

## Dopamine and Cortisol

We should seek to minimize the debilitating stress (distress) that releases cortisol and maximize motivating stress (eustress) that releases dopamine. That sentence is a mouthful, right?

Let's break that down and define our terms.

What is Dopamine? From Psychology Today, "Dopamine is a neurotransmitter that helps control the brain's reward and pleasure centers. Dopamine also helps regulate movement and emotional responses, and it enables us not only to see rewards, but to take action to move toward them."

So when you engage in activities that release dopamine, the classic example being exercise, you feel happier and more motivated as a result.

What is Cortisol? Cortisol is commonly referred to as "the stress hormone". It affects everything from your immune system to your digestive ability to your reproductive system. It's a mood-altering, early warning alarm system that triggers powerful changes throughout your body and mind.

The Mayo Clinic reports that, "The long-term activation of the stress-response system – and the subsequent over-exposure to cortisol and other stress hormones – can disrupt almost all your body's processes. This puts you at increased risk of numerous health problems, including:

- Anxiety
- Depression
- Digestive problems
- Heart disease
- Sleep problems

- Weight gain
- Memory and concentration impairment

That's why it's so important to learn healthy ways to cope with the stressors in your life."

I quoted the Mayo Clinic at length there because the list is so long and the effects so profound that I didn't want you to think I was just making it up to sell books! The effects of prolonged stress exposure on your physical and mental ability to function really are that bad.

This is why it's so very important to learn to develop a calm and focused mind.

## Your Nervous System

Your automatic nervous system (ANS) does everything from regulating blood flow to maintaining breathing to keeping your heart beating, all without conscious intent. It keeps you alive without your even having to think about it.

A subset of the ANS is your SNS or sympathetic nervous system. This is what controls your stress response and what you'll need to learn to manage in order to stress less.

When a perceived threat emerges, the SNS releases cortisol and adrenaline into your body, putting you in a state of hyper-vigilance and triggering the fight-or-flight response.

When the threat is real and actionable, an impending car crash for instance, this burst of energy results in a quick response that can save your life. It's a very effective defense system when our lives actually need defending.

More typically though, in our modern society, the stress response is triggered by the equivalent of a car alarm rather than a car crash. There is no threat to fight, no impending disaster to run from, and no release for the cortisol and adrenaline that's produced. It just ends up building up and interfering with your parasympathetic nervous system's (PNS) ability to rest and digest.

The job of your PNS is to conserve energy when you're not in danger. This is the body's natural resting state and it's the balance between these two systems of tension and relaxation that allows us to function optimally. Get too far out of balance for too long and your immune system will suffer. You'll wear down and break down. There needs to be both tension and release.

# 9

# Proactive vs Reactive Responses

*"To the mind that is still, the whole universe surrenders"*
**– Lao Tzu**

Human beings are hardwired to experience the fight or flight response in the face of real or perceived threats and have been for thousands of years. Also called "the stress response", it evolved to alert us to the presence of danger. An early warning system that could save your life, it exists to protect us.

Thousands of years ago, before we became agrarian societies, staying in one place with indoor heating and plumbing and pantries full of food, we were hunter gatherers. Physiologically, we are very much the same creatures today as we were back then.

When we had to go out and hunt for our food, dangers were everywhere. Sometimes the predator would become the prey and that "food" would attack us!

Something as small as the snap of a twig could signal an attack. The stress response kicked in, our adrenaline became heightened, senses more alert, ready to fight or flee. Attack or retreat. Your very life was on the line. In that environment the stress response is life saving.

If a mountain lion is above you on a hill and is going to jump down and attack you, you either need to fight for your life or run for your life. That triggers the stress response and is why it's

# Fight or Flight Response

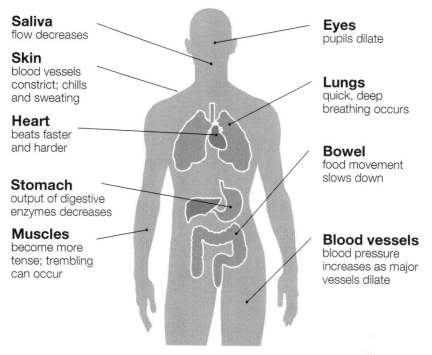

**Saliva**
flow decreases

**Skin**
blood vessels
constrict; chills
and sweating

**Heart**
beats faster
and harder

**Stomach**
output of digestive
enzymes decreases

**Muscles**
become more
tense; trembling
can occur

**Eyes**
pupils dilate

**Lungs**
quick, deep
breathing occurs

**Bowel**
food movement
slows down

**Blood vessels**
blood pressure
increases as major
vessels dilate

called "fight or flight". It's not a decision. It's a highly adrenalized, automatically produced response to stress.

In today's modern society, that's still what happens in our bodies when we get stressed out because we're very much the same creatures now as we were back then. We tense up. We react. The more stressed out we become, the more overreactive we become.

The fight or flight reaction was a life saving response when our ancestors either had to hunt to survive or become hunted themselves. But fight or flight responses rarely make sense today because there's no one to fight and nowhere to run. So the stress hormones that are produced when the fight or flight response is triggered have nowhere to go but build up inside you until they create a constant state of agitation. It's an unfortunate byproduct of living under constant pressure.

Imagine you're trapped in stop-and-go traffic on the freeway, and you're late to an important appointment. Your cellphone is ringing and shaking, and people are pushing in and out of lanes all around you, trying to get an edge. You are definitely going to be late and to make matters worse, you got in an argument before you left home.

Stress, stress, stress, stress, stress, stress, STRESS!

So what happens with all that pressure that you've been suppressing? It just builds up inside of you until you feel like you've got to find a way to vent it before you blow, right?

When left unresolved, the tendency to cope through activities that trigger your pleasure centers (such as overeating, smoking, shopping, sleeping, and mindlessly scrolling through endless social media posts) can compound the negative effects and result in an overall level of unproductivity and even illness.

So how do you let off steam? If you don't know how to vent in a productive, proactive way, it builds up. It builds up, and you want to release it through an emotional outburst, but what most people do is stuff it back down with food. Comfort eating. Emotional eating. Any wonder there's a link between stress and weight gain?

All that cortisol and adrenaline have to go somewhere!

You become saturated with adrenaline when you're constantly stressed. When there's no place for it to go, most people stuff it down into their waistline. They attempt to stimulate the pleasure centers of the brain with snacks, cakes, candies, potato chips, ice cream, chocolate, and more. Ultimately that either makes a person sick or obese.

This stress response is really overkill for most situations but exists just the same within us all. We've been hardwired to react. But we're much more effective human beings when we're proactive rather than reactive.

The constant triggering of the stress response degrades the quality of our lives without adding any appreciable benefit. It's like a crossed wire that won't allow a light to turn on and off but only remain burning energy in an empty room.

We need to rewire that switch so it only turns on when there's a good reason and preserve energy when there is not. You will be just as safe without the worry and actually be more responsive to legitimate stressors when they do occur. Relaxed, focused, and proactive is the goal as opposed to stressed, unfocused, and reactive.

# 10

# Your Stress Test

*"Know thyself"*
**– Ancient Greek Delphic Maxim**

Let's assess your current level of stress because the first step in making any meaningful change is becoming aware of the problem that needs to be addressed.

Stress manifests itself through a wide variety of symptoms. These symptoms can be broken down into four distinct categories: Emotional, Self-Talk, Behavioral, and Physical. Give yourself the following test to assess your own stress level.

Higher stress levels lead to increased incidences of conflict and illness and lower levels of focus and productivity. The first step in reducing stress and alleviating these symptoms is to identify the level of stress that exists and acknowledge the importance of addressing it.

Once identified, coping mechanisms can be implemented.

Let's start your Stress Test self assessment.

# SECTION I: Emotional Symptoms

Check off the feelings you have on a day-to-day basis. Write in your score in the box at the bottom of the page.

- Mood swings                                        _____

- Feelings of guilt                                  _____

- Feelings of tension                               _____

- Feelings of anger                                 _____

- No enthusiasm                                     _____

- Feeling out of control                            _____

- Feelings of helplessness                          _____

- Poor concentration                                _____

- Feelings of shame                                 _____

- Feeling anxious                                    _____

- Becoming more cynical                             _____

- Decrease in confidence/self-esteem                _____

TOTAL SECTION I:

# SECTION II: Self-Talk Symptoms

Check off the thoughts you have on a day-to-day basis. Write in your score in the box at the bottom of the page.

- "No one understands"                                 ......................

- "I keep forgetting where I put things"          ......................

- "I can't cope"                                              ......................

- "I am a failure"                                            ......................

- "I don't know what to do"                           ......................

- "What is the point?"                                    ......................

- "Why is everyone upset with me?"              ......................

- "I don't seem to be able to get ahead"       ......................

- "I should be able to handle all of this"        ......................

- "Why does this always happen to me?"        ......................

TOTAL SECTION II:

# SECTION III: Behavioral Symptoms

Check off the behaviors you have noticed in yourself on a day-to-day basis. Write in your score in the box at the bottom of the page.

- Drop in work performance                    _____

- More accident prone                    _____

- Too busy to relax                    _____

- Poor judgment                    _____

- Inability to express feelings                    _____

- Overreacting                    _____

- Poor time management                    _____

- Increase in drinking and/or smoking                    _____

- Overeating/loss of appetite                    _____

- Change in sleeping patterns                    _____

- Withdrawing from family and friends                    _____

TOTAL SECTION III:

# SECTION IV: Physical Symptoms

Use this checklist to evaluate your physical condition. Check off the physical symptoms of stress that you are experiencing.

- Sleep problems/tiredness          _____

- Headaches          _____

- Nausea          _____

- Tightness in chest          _____

- Indigestion          _____

- Breathlessness          _____

- Muscle twitches          _____

- Aches and pains          _____

- Skin conditions          _____

- Weight loss or weight gain          _____

- Reoccurring illness or allergies          _____

- Chest pain or palpitations          _____

- Constipation/diarrhea          _____

- Women only – change in menstrual cycle _____

- Men only – change in reaction to menstrual cycle :-)          _____

TOTAL SECTION IV:

# RESULTS PAGE

Please write in your total score from each section of this test. Add them up and see below for your stress assessment.

TOTAL FROM SECTION I         _____

TOTAL FROM SECTION II        _____

TOTAL FROM SECTION III       _____

TOTAL FROM SECTION IV       _____

GRAND TOTAL:                                    

# Results:

**0-4 symptoms:** You are doing fine.

**5-8 symptoms:** You are experiencing mild stress, and you should learn how to manage your stress before it gets worse.

**9-12 symptoms:** You are experiencing moderate stress. You need to use stress management techniques daily and make some key changes in your life before it impacts your health.

**13 + symptoms:** The higher your score, the more urgent it is for you to take action to reduce your stress. At this level it's important that you take steps to reduce your stress immediately. Please consult your physician and share these results.

## Coping With Stress

We've identified where you are now. It's helpful to get that baseline in place before we start discussing solutions.

We can't entirely avoid stress, but we can learn to reduce our exposure to it, improve our response to it, and increase our immunity to it.

Those are really the only three ways to effectively manage stress.
1. Reduce your exposure to stress producing stimuli
2. Improve your response to stressful situations
3. Increase your immunity to stress

Over the next few chapters, I'm going to challenge you to make some changes to your daily routine in each of those areas. Even small changes can add up to big results.

Keep an open mind and imagine what's possible. Imagine the person you can become. Act "as if" you're already doing these things. Project yourself into that reality. Then day by day, make it so. Little by little you'll become better, faster, stronger. You'll become Kanye West! Just kidding. You'll become a higher functioning version of yourself. Take a deep breath and let's dive in!

# 11

# Increase Immunity:
## Diet & Exercise

*"The best six doctors anywhere, And no one can deny it,*
*Are sunshine, water, rest, and air, Exercise and diet"*
– Wayne Fields

## Diet

This is the big one for many people. They may not realize that stress is causing their weight gain, but emotional eating and overeating are classic coping methods.

When you eat to feel better emotionally that's called, wait for it… emotional eating. It's a common way to cope with stress that can have devastating effects on your weight and self-confidence.

Ever look down to find your hand rummaging around at the bottom of a bag of chips and you don't even remember eating them? Or find yourself polishing off a pint of ice cream without even thinking about it or really enjoying it? That's emotional eating.

You feel bad so you eat and that leads to weight gain which makes you feel lethargic and depressed, so you eat more to feel better, and the vicious cycle continues.

Let's do this quick exercise to discover if you're prone to emotional eating. Put one hand up in the air, it doesn't matter which one, we're not taking an oath. Feel what it feels like to feel hunger in your body now. Where do you feel that? It's a little bit different for everybody.

Now put your hand on the spot where you physically feel hunger and notice where your hand is. The higher up your hand is, the closer to your heart it is, the more prone you are to emotional eating. The lower down it is, the closer it is to your stomach. But if there's a feeling of emptiness up near your heart, it's not going to be filled by food. The more you're aware of that psychosomatic response, the more you're empowered to do something about it.

The first step is to journal your eating habits for a week. See where you're at and get a realistic picture of your consumption.

When you are at your ideal weight it puts less stress on your physical frame and results in more energy for productive pursuits. And when you feel better about your weight it improves your emotional state, your self-confidence, and your motivation to get things done. You feel more successful and in control of your life and have the energy to attack the day.

So, get ready for the simplest diet advice ever: Don't.

Diets aren't particularly effective for 90% of the people who use them. And when you go on a diet and fail to reach or maintain your goal, it reinforces a pattern of failure, which is unhelpful.

Instead, make the conscious decision to change your eating habits to maximize your health and longevity.

What follows is not a diet. There are no restrictions on how much you eat or when you eat it and there is no end goal in mind. My *10 Point Eating Action Plan* is a lifestyle choice that you follow because you've decided that your life is worth living to its fullest potential.

Of course, you should always consult your physician before starting any diet or exercise program. It's a good idea to get a check up anyway so you know where you're starting from.

That said, if you're ready to make a change and clean up your eating habits today, then here's what I suggest…

# Diet

When I'm at home and not traveling to give presentations, I eat the exact same thing for three out of four meals a day. This saves on prep time, decision making, and grocery shopping so that I can focus on other things. It's also very healthy.

People claim not to have time to eat right so they consume fast food or packaged, processed foods high in calories and low in nutrition. But when you systemize your eating routine it takes very little time to prepare and the benefits to your health are enormous.

Here's what I eat every single day:

### Breakfast

1 scoop of isolated whey protein powder (no lactose or sugar)
1 cup of coconut milk
1 teaspoon of almond butter
1 banana or berries or both

Put them all in a blender and mix for a few seconds. Drink. Move on to the next activity. That's it. Takes about a minute and a half to make a high-protein breakfast that will give you abundant energy, leave you feeling full until lunch, be easy to digest, and is so simple to make that even a kid can do it.

### Lunch

I take all the vegetables I can find, chop them up, add a protein source (I like chicken, tuna, or salmon), throw in some beans so it digests more slowly, and top it all off with an oil and vinegar-based dressing. Sometimes I eat two of these. Why not? They're just vegetables and some protein. No need to count calories or restrict portions.

Lunch takes about 5 minutes to prepare and is the biggest meal of the day.

**Dinner**
I follow the guidance in the 10 Point Eating Plan listed below and allow for some dietary variety in my day.

**Nighttime Snack**
A couple of hours before retiring for the evening, I take all the fruits I can find, chop them up, and enjoy a small fruit salad with my wife. That provides a sweet ending to the day in more ways than one :-)

**Drink**
Water. Occasionally a black coffee or tea. Don't drink calories!

And that's it. It's not complicated, time consuming, or expensive. The preparation involved is minimal and the nutritive value is excellent. Nothing is packaged, processed, bagged, or boxed except for the protein powder. Everything is comprised of real, naturally occurring food in it's whole form. There is no sugar or dairy and minimal carbohydrates.

There's isn't even any cooking involved on a daily basis. All protein is purchased, prepared, portioned, and refrigerated once a week. Everything else is fresh.

I've been eating this way for a long time and I can tell you that after a brief initial adjustment period, it feels great! Lots of clean burning energy throughout the day, no cravings, and a fit physique.

# Your 10 Point Eating Action Plan

1.  Drink water and unsweetened coffee and tea. Mostly water, though, as coffee and tea are diuretics and will leave you feeling more thirsty.

2.  Since the brain has a hard time differentiating between hunger and thirst, get in the habit of drinking a glass of water 10-20 minutes before each meal. This will act as a natural appetite suppressant.

3.  Eat slowly and mindfully. In other words, be grateful for the food on your plate and chew your food slowly. It takes 20 minutes for the feeling of "full" to travel from your stomach to your brain, so when you slow down your rate of eating not only do you enjoy your food more but you give yourself a chance to stop eating before you become painfully stuffed.

4.  Reduce or eliminate the whites: salt, dairy, refined carbohydrates, and sugar. You'll still get plenty of salt in your diet if you stop adding it to your food and you'll cut down on water retention and your risk of hypertension in the process. Dairy is hard to digest and saps your energy. When you stop eating dairy, as I did over 10 years ago, it cuts a lot of fat and calories out of your food. It also cuts out a lot of unhealthy foods like pizza and ice cream (which I'm embarrassed to say I consumed on an almost daily basis all throughout college). Refined carbohydrates include foods like bread and potatoes (including chips and french fries). There's a reason athletes carbo load. Are you an athlete? If not, you don't need these foods as sources of fuel.

And finally, sugar. Sugar is in so many food products that you would be shocked to discover how much you consume on a daily basis. Some form of sugar is in practically every food that's boxed, bagged, canned, processed, packaged, or refined. When I decided to eliminate sugar from my diet in the summer of 2014, I'd just consumed an entire basket of "fun-sized" candy bars backstage between my shows. I figured it would be easier to simply eliminate it entirely than try to cut it down. I knew that, like most people, if I had a little, I'd be very likely to have a lot. But if I never had any in the first place it wouldn't be nearly as tempting. And guess what? It worked!

Except for a few passing moments (like when I opened my son's trick-or-treat candy for him and held it inches from my mouth!), I've found it very easy to avoid sugar. Just read the labels at the grocery store or, better yet, buy real food and make it yourself. The result of eliminating sugar from my diet has been profound.

I didn't consider myself overweight to begin with, yet I lost over 20 pounds in the first 3 months alone without changing anything else about my exercise or eating. That bears repeating: I didn't even consider myself overweight and still managed to lose 20 pounds in 3 months just by cutting sugar out of my diet. Amazing!

5.  If you want something sweet, eat fruit. Fruit is wrapped in fiber and it's naturally occurring sugars will absorb into your bloodstream at a much slower and more manageable rate than refined sugars. But don't have fruit juice! When you separate the juice from the fiber

you increase its rate of absorption, spike your blood sugar and insulin levels, and throw your body chemistry out of balance. Just stick to the whole fruit and you'll be fine.

6. Eat all the vegetables you want. Eat them raw in a salad, as a snack, or cooked as a side with your protein-rich meal. Have as many vegetables as you want throughout the day. Vegetables are okay to juice, by the way. They're rich in vitamins and will give you plenty of fiber to help detox your body from all the foods you won't be eating anymore.

7. Eat some protein at every meal but especially at breakfast. Start your day with energy-building protein in your favorite form. Keep your glycemic index low. And notice how that sets the tone for your appetite throughout the day. Cravings will disappear and you'll have the clean burning fuel you need to be effective until the next meal. Food is fuel – treat it as such.

8. If you need a snack between meals and want a break from fruits and vegetables, have a few nuts. But not too many. I've made that mistake on cross country flights on my way to events and it can leave you feeling bloated and uncomfortable. A handful of nuts is all you need to make it to the next meal.

9. Throw out everything in your house that doesn't meet the preceding guidelines. It's much easier to resist temptation when it isn't there.

10. Keep doing it. Every day. This is not a diet, it's a lifestyle. You don't do it to reach a goal but to live a healthier life.

It might take a few days to get used to these new eating patterns, but within a few weeks it will feel normal and very worthwhile. You'll certainly have to start shopping differently. It's no more expensive to eat this way because you're eliminating processed and packaged foods. And the health benefits are enormous.

You'll notice there's no calorie counting. It's not necessary. It's really very simple and once you get used to it you'll notice that the foods you do eat start tasting better.

If you ever decide to have packaged, processed food (say you're at a party and you're hungry and that's all that's available), you'll notice you can taste the chemicals in the snacks and that the deserts are unpleasantly sweet.

Your taste buds will recalibrate pretty quickly. It's surprising.

Best of all, you'll never need to be hungry. Eat all the whole fruits, vegetables, and proteins you like in a slow and mindful way. I often have two salads for lunch. Why not? A little chicken or salmon on top (or beans, lentils, avocados, chia seeds, nuts, or seitan if you're a vegetarian) and you've got yourself a delicious, nutritious meal.

Follow the advice given in the old adage: "Eat breakfast like a king, lunch like a prince, and dinner like a pauper."

Start your day with a burst of power from a protein rich breakfast. And make sure your dinner is smaller than your lunch. Food is fuel and if all you're doing between dinner and bed time is sitting around, then you don't need much of it. No need to have it sitting in your stomach, turning to fat while you sleep. If you're hungry, have a few nuts and a glass of water and call it a night.

Now go throw out all your diet books!

## Exercise

When most people think of exercise, they think of joining a gym. They imagine themselves working up a sweat, doing cardio and pumping iron, maybe even taking some classes.

"This is it! I'm finally gonna get in shape! Just look at all this equipment! Here's my credit card."

So they fork over the membership fee and commit themselves to this exercise regimen for the duration of the contract. And these contracts tend to be long and hard to cancel because the reality is that the vast majority of gym members rarely if ever step foot in the place. That's why the typical gym loses over half its members each year – because when your contract is up you see how much you've paid to NOT exercise.

Working out is hard and takes time and most people simply don't do it, regardless of their intentions when joining their local gym. To counter this trend, gyms have started adding fun-themed events to bring their members in the doors for other reasons. Bagel breakfasts and pizza nights for instance. Never mind the irony of carbo loading after you've just worked out. The objective is to have you remember that you occasionally went to the gym when your membership runs out so it'll seem like a good idea to renew since you actually did use it.

Does this seem beneficial to you? Not to me either.

There is an exception to this kind of a gym and that's the relatively new phenomenon of those based around a group exercise program. I'm not talking about generalized classes. I mean a hybrid between having a private trainer and no trainer. This format provides variety, motivation, oversight and guidance. Not to mention the competitive aspect endemic to a group coaching situation.

I don't know about you, but I'm compelled to push myself to be at the top of that board at the end of each class. There are several such types of high intensity group exercise programs gaining in popularity around the country. The one my wife and I love going to is called Orange Theory Fitness. It offers high intensity interval training that sets a powerful energy level throughout the rest of the day.

The only downside is the expense. It costs about ten times more than a big box gym. Because of the high level of participation, there are effectively far fewer people subsidizing our memberships. Traditional gyms can offer low monthly fees because they sign up many times their physical capacity to accommodate the members. If their members don't show up then all those inactive members essentially pay for the active members to work out.

In the new group training type gyms, you have to make an appointment to reserve your space. Practically everyone shows up, and they all get guidance and feedback from trainers, so the fees need to be  much higher. And believe me, they are. Worth every penny but beyond the reach of most people.

Thankfully, there's another way to achieve many of the benefits of daily exercise for just a few dollars and get guidance and feedback from something you already own. What is it? What can replace many of the functions of that expensive or unused gym membership? Wait for it... Your phone.

There are now free or extremely inexpensive apps on your smart phone that can help you achieve many of the same benefits as going to the gym for a fraction of the time and expense. Here are just a few examples:

- 7 Minute Workout Apps (calisthenics)
- Yoga and stretching apps
- Pedometer Apps


Start with a $1 pedometer app on your smart phone. Or a $5 physical pedometer if you're still using a beeper ;-)

The average American walks 8,000 steps a day. Even if you increase that to 10,000 steps, that's an extra mile.

In the South, such as where I live in Florida, 6,000 steps a day is more typical.

That lack of physical activity leads to weight gain and eventually to your body shutting down. It's representative of a sedentary life style, leads to a lot of health issues, and mindset issues, too. This is because when you move around you release dopamine, stimulate your endorphins, and you just feel better.

## Ambulation Exercise

For the first week, simply log how much you are walking on a daily basis. If you're like most people in the United States, you take about 8,000 steps a day.

For the second week, get to 10,000 steps. Park a little bit further away from the door, take the stairs instead of the elevator, go for a walk. You'll find that when you break it up, it's not that difficult to walk those extra 2,000 steps.

For the third week and beyond, maintain. What we've just done is added an extra mile of walking to your day, every day. That can have an enormous impact on your ability to cope with stress, your ability to focus, your mood, your mindset, and your weight. You're moving your body, you're stimulating your metabolism, and you're becoming a more efficient burner of fuel. It's just an all around good idea.

Can you commit right now to doing that? Go ahead and make that commitment to yourself today. Challenge yourself to do it and you will begin to see enormous benefits from this one simple activity over time. Among other things, exercising increases your ability to focus and proactively respond to pressure. A little exercise can go a long way.

# 12

# 10 Tips to Work Well Under Pressure

*"It is not the mountain we conquer, but ourselves."*
**– Sir Edmund Hillary**

Here are 10 simple steps you can take each day to reduce stress and work well under pressure. Whenever you're feeling overwhelmed and in need of a quick fix, do at least three things on this list to get back on track and in control of your responses.

## 1. Stand Up and STRETCH!
Taking a minute to stand up and stretch at your desk is a great stress reliever. It takes your mind off what you are working on and helps get your blood flowing.

## 2. Breathe Slowly and Deeply
When you feel ready to explode, take a minute, close your eyes and begin breathing slowly and deeply. In through the nose and out through the mouth. Whisper the sound "ahhh" when you exhale. Do this slowly several times until your emotions regain equilibrium.

## 3. Do One Thing at a Time
When we try to do multiple things at once, most of the time we end up not doing any of them well. Take one task at a time, give it your full attention until completion, and you will be less stressed and more productive.

## 4. Have An Attitude of Gratitude

Sometimes we can get so caught up in our daily lives that we forget about the big picture. Take a minute and write down who and what you are grateful for. It will calm you and improve your attitude.

## 5. Laugh at Yourself

Laughter is great medicine. If you can laugh at something you've done, you won't take yourself so seriously and will realize that we're all human and make misteaks. ;-)

## 6. Limit Your Exposure to Email, TV, and Social Media

Only open your email client and social media accounts at scheduled intervals. And turn off the TV whenever possible. You'll find it easier to focus on your work by minimizing those stress producing distractions.

## 7. Go Outside For a Walk

Take a few minutes out of your lunch or coffee break to take a walk. The fresh air will revitalize you, the exercise is good for your body, and getting away from your daily routine for a moment will allow you to return in a better frame of mind.

## 8. Get Up Earlier in the Morning

Getting up even 15 minutes earlier can help with the hurried race to get out the door in the morning. If you start your day right and on time, chances are good that the rest of your day will follow the same pattern. Be 10 minutes early to every appointment and consider that 10 minutes early is on time.

## 9. Make a List. Then Use It.

Making a list at night of what you need to do the following day puts your tasks in perspective so they don't become overwhelming. Use your list and check off what you've completed. It's a good feeling to see what you have accomplished. Keep the list small so you can do it all. Just what you can fit on a post-it note.

## 10. Use Meditation to Relax

Guided meditation is a quick and easy way to relax, refocus, and reenergize yourself. You can learn more about how to tap into this powerful stress reduction technique with your free download at www.findingfocusbook.com

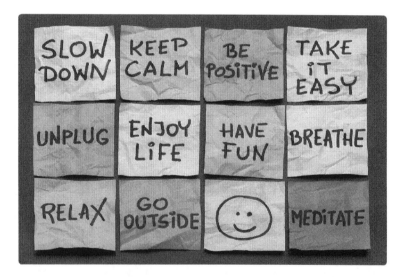

# PART 3

## FOCUS ON YOUR PRODUCTIVITY

# 13

# 21 Tips To Increase Productivity

*"If we all did the things we are capable of doing, we would literally astound ourselves."* – **Thomas Alva Edison**

So far, we've addressed the emotional, psychological, and physiological components that will enable you to find greater focus. Now let's dive into the specific productivity techniques that will help you to tune out the noise and work well under pressure. With that in mind, here are 21 quick tips you can implement right now.

## 1. Limit Your Commitments

Focus on doing a few things well and be careful not to overextend yourself. That requires that you to be selective and limit your commitments.

We only have a limited number of hours in the day to get things done and make progress toward our goals. An increase in productive time is really the value that you get from limiting your commitments. So circle the wagons around your current projects before you start saying yes to even more.

It's okay to say no. As the saying goes, "If you want to get something done, give it to a busy person". The theory being that if they're already busy, that's because they can handle the work. But if that person is you, then it's important to put limits on what you are willing to accept.

We all have limited time and energy. If you're wearing yourself out saying yes to everything you're asked to do, then narrow your focus to just those things that will produce the most value and limit your commitments to everything else.

I realize that the common advice is to do exactly the opposite of that, say yes to everything, every opportunity, say yes to life! But what happens when you do that is you end up going in lots of different directions at once, fracturing your focus, and running out of time and energy to do anything well.

It's important to say Yes to people and Yes to life and Yes to opportunities. But when those opportunities take your time and destroy your focus, then you have to know when to say "Enough is enough". Today is that day.

Commit to focusing on your current work commitments and getting them under control before expanding out even more. That may mean declining some opportunities in the short term. That may even mean saying no to people for right now.

It's all right to say "No". You're the most important person in your own life, after all, because if you're not able to give to yourself first then you won't have enough time and energy left over to give to others. Many people mistakenly believe that they need to give to others first, but ultimately we need to give to ourselves first if there is to be anything left over to give to others.

Don't worry, eventually you will have mastered the techniques in this book and find that you have more time and energy then you know what to do with. You'll be able to begin saying "Yes" to those requests again. But first you've got to focus on your preexisting commitments so you can do them well.

Each time you say "Yes" to someone and take on another commitment, it weighs down on your psyche until that commitment is either fulfilled or abandoned. So start limiting your commitments and say "Yes" to others less often.

When you do say "Yes," then really mean it. Your word is your bond and accepting a commitment is a promise to fulfill it. In the remaining instances where you commit to work beyond what you're already doing, resolve to follow through on that promise and do it well.

Anything worth doing is worth doing well but to make that happen consistently requires narrowing the focus of your work. Instead of continuously expanding your commitments, let's start this process by narrowing your focus on doing your own work well.

Say yes to yourself now so you have a greater capacity to say yes to others later.

## 2. Do Your 3 Most Important Things First

Each night, before you go to bed, write the three most important things you can do the following day on a post-it note. Don't put them in your phone, actually write them out by hand on a post-it note and put that on your screen so you see it as soon as you sit down to work the next morning.

Lots of people make to-do lists, but they mistakenly believe they can do more than time and energy allow, so at the end of each day they just transfer those unfinished items over to another list along with all the additional things they have to do. Eventually that just gets to be overwhelming and unproductive.

Identify the top three things you can do that will produce the biggest results, create the most value, or move you forward the fastest. Three actions you can take that will be the most meaningful. Then write those three things on your post-it note right before you go to bed.

Get them out of your head so you can rest and let your subconscious mind begin processing the best way to complete those tasks while you sleep.

The following day, do those things first. Right after your

morning routine. It's a great feeling to cross them off one by one and then toss that note in the trash before lunch. If you get nothing else done that day but those three things you will have moved your life and your career forward.

Even if you only get one or two things of that caliber done each day you'll find that over the course of weeks and months and years, you've accomplished quite a lot. It's not necessary to do a lot of things every day. It is necessary that the things that you do have impact and create value.

If all you're doing is running errands and answering emails and returning calls, you're not really moving forward in your life. If you put the three most important things on a list like this, do them, and make a new one every night, then you will find that it's very easy to get ahead. Progress will occur automatically.

Put a stack of Post-It notes next to your bed so that before you go to sleep tonight you can write down the three most important things you need to do tomorrow. Do that every day. You'll find that you'll sleep better at night and be more rested when you wake up in the morning. When you wake up, it will be with a sense of purpose because you'll know exactly what you need to focus on that day.

The cumulative effect of just focusing on your three most important tasks each day is truly transformative. It creates momentum and narrows your focus like a laser.

## 3. Prioritize

It's become common for people to waste their entire morning by getting up and immediately scrolling through social media, checking the news, and lingering over their email – these things don't move us forward in life.

Instead, get in the habit of consulting your Post-It note to-do list. You should already have one of these – now we're going to make sure that you're taking action on the most important thing on that list first. This is really the easiest way to accomplish more by doing less.

Let's narrow your focus even more. Just do the single most important thing on that list, the first thing in the morning after you've eaten a protein rich breakfast and readied yourself for work, while you've got time and energy on your side.

Once that's completed, check your email. Once that's completed, do another one of those tasks on your post-it-note. Break up those three most important tasks in order of priority.

There is a famous story about a professor that was lecturing a class with a mason jar and a bunch of rocks. Here's the short version:

Basically he puts all the big rocks in the jar first and asks the class if it's full. They say, "Yes." Then he puts some pebbles in and they fill in the spaces between the big rocks and he again asks the class if it's full. Again they say, "Yes." Then he puts in some sand and fills in the spaces between the smaller rocks. You get the idea.

The point is that if you do the big important things first, you have lots of room left over for all the smaller ones. But if you fill up all your time (as represented by the mason jar) with the small tasks (as represented by the sand) then you won't have any room left for those big rocks, the things that get us ahead in life.

Start making it a habit to prioritize and focus on the most important things first. Just this one tip will eliminate a lot of overwhelm because the work that remains produces less value than the work you already did. Everything else just isn't as important, by definition. This is an empowering concept that creates energy, forward momentum, and a sense of accomplishment.

Start prioritizing where you spend your time – because time is a nonrenewable resource and the most precious gift we can give.

## 4. Whiteboard

Use a whiteboard as your second to-do list. This is different than your 3 item Post-it Note list. This is the place to put everything else you have to do. Get that information out of your head and off your phone and away from your desktop. Put it up there in a big, easy to read fashion that gives you a sense of all your pending tasks at a glance.

I visually represent this by dividing the giant whiteboard on my wall into Present tasks (on the left) and Future tasks (on the right). If it doesn't get written down on that white board, then it doesn't need to be done by you personally. Everything not on that whiteboard or on your 3 item Post-it note can be delegated, outsourced, or eliminated (see tip #10).

If you don't have a big whiteboard on your wall, go out and get one today. Draw a vertical line down the center of the board. Write "Present" or "Current" on the top left and "Future" on the top right. Then populate that whiteboard with everything you personally need to get done. Draw horizontal lines across the board to group tasks into projects. Then take a moment to enjoy yourself every time you wipe one of those tasks off the board. It's a fun and organizationally intelligent thing to do.

## 5. Link Music To Work

Music can trigger focus when songs are constantly linked to specific activities. In the chapter on meditation at the beginning of this book I mention that I listen to the same song in the shower every day. It's actually been the exact same song for years now and I listen to that song at no other time. It's that familiarity and reputation that creates a meditative zone-like state. And because it's 9 minutes long I always know I can get ready in under 10 minutes. I never feel rushed. Just move in tempo with the music and before I know it the task is done. You can apply this principle to all kinds of work.

When you link music to specific activities, it creates greater focus. For instance, I've listened to the same playlist while writing all three of my books. In case you were wondering, it's primarily comprised of the album *Underwater Sunlight* by Tangerine Dream. Whenever I hear that music I know it's time to write and so I do. The words begin to flow automatically.

In order to keep this musical trigger active, I make sure never to listen to this particular playlist unless I'm already sitting at my laptop and ready to write. It would diffuse the music's effectiveness on my subconscious to listen to it at any other time. You can do this, too.

Select specific music to listen to corresponding with each type of focused activity you wish to engage in. The music should be different for each type of task. Technically, baroque music at 60 beats per minute is best for focused concentration, but you can certainly expand to different genres if that suits your taste. The trick is to be consistent about linking it to specific activities and to reinforce that every single time you do it.

Whenever I'm listening to a project that requires manual labor, such as yard work or a home improvement project, I listen to The Beatles, *Abbey Road*. I've been consistent about that for more than 20 years so the effect is instantaneous. I hear that music and get to work. It puts me in the desired zone. What music does that for you? And can you commit to only listening to it when you do a certain type of activity, every single time you do that activity, so you can trigger and maintain focus? It's amazingly effective.

In the case of my writing, I literally never get writer's block and I attribute that to this technique which I've applied to the same music selection since college. The words just flow. I'm listening to it right now, in fact.

When I'm done writing I will turn that playlist off and not listen to it again until the next time I write. It may take you a little time to establish a link between your music selection and the type of work you associate it to but eventually the effect will kick in and it will result in a kind of effortless effectiveness that's incredibly gratifying.

To make the process of selecting the music easier, I've shared my Pandora playlist as one of the bonuses on the website. I'm continuously tweaking it to create better flow and focus. It really locks me in while I'm doing daily computer work and I think it'll have the same effect on you.

Listen to it now at www.findingfocusbook.com/music

## 6. Use The Pomodoro Technique

Oh this is a good one! If you've never heard of the Pomodoro technique or aren't yet using it on a daily basis, you are really missing out on an excellent way to improve your focus. I love it. I'm using it right now while I write this!

Work expands to fill the time allotted to it. Therefore, you can accomplish more by limiting the time you give yourself to do it. The Pomodoro technique puts tight time limits on your activities which helps you to accomplish those tasks faster because you're in a race with yourself to get them done.

The Pomodoro technique was developed in the early 1990s by Francesco Cirillo. He found that he could focus intensely by using a simple tomato-shaped kitchen timer – the word "pomodoro" means tomato in Italian.

Here's how to use this simple, effective time management technique:

1.  Select the most important task you can do at the moment
2.  Set a timed interval for 25 minutes
3.  Work on that task continuously until the timer rings. The sound of the ticking clock will push your productivity forward. As the sound intensifies toward the end so will your output.

4. Take a 5 minute break and then repeat the process. Every 4 intervals take a longer break of 20-30 minutes.

That's it. And let me tell you, it works wonders for locking in your focus and producing massive results in short periods of time.

The rest periods deserve discussion as well, and we'll do that in the next tip. In the meantime, get yourself a kitchen timer that ticks or use a Pomodoro app on your smart phone. You'll be amazed at the results.

# 7. Schedule In Rest Periods

No one can work around the clock without suffering consequences to their health and the quality of their output. Working harder and for longer periods of time produces diminishing returns.

Working in a more focused fashion for short periods of time maximizes the value of your output. Build in rest periods after short bursts of focused productivity.

Time your work periods using the Pomodoro technique outlined in the previous section and then step away for 5 minutes. Either close your eyes and practice breathing deeply or go for a walk and move your body. In both cases, the shift in focus will allow you to return to your work refreshed and rejuvenated.

After running this sequence four times, take a longer break of 20-30 minutes. Even though you'll be taking lots of rest periods, the level of your productivity will go through the roof because the timed intervals will keep you focused on the task at hand and working intensely.

Rest periods are crucial to maintaining the quality of your work during periods of productivity. Getting things done is less important than getting the most meaningful things done well. In order to do that throughout the day and stay healthy, you need to schedule in rest periods. They're just as important as work periods. Together they create sustainable balance.

# 8. Speed Up Input

If your focus is on improving productivity, then consider this: the more time you spend taking things in, the less time you have for putting things out.

Nothing can kill focus faster than filling your day with watching, listening to, and reading things that other people have produced. If you want to focus on your own work, then you have to minimize the time you spend focusing on the work of others.

The more content you consume, the less time and inclination you have to create. That's one of the benefits of cutting down on or eliminating TV, social media, and the news. It frees up a lot of extra time to make things happen yourself instead of passively watching what other people have accomplished.

That said, we all have things we need to watch, listen to, and read on a daily basis. Some of these things we do for pleasure and that activity should be relished not rushed. But for everything else, here's how to cut the time you spend consuming other people's work in half.

### Videos

Have you ever thought to yourself that people take too long to get to the point in training and how-to videos? I watch a lot of these and the information can be very helpful but I used to find myself scanning through them to get to the relevant information. No more! There's a more efficient way to consume this kind of content.

Inexpensive software exists that allows you to speed up online and downloaded videos without making people sound like chipmunks. I now regularly watch these kinds of videos at 2x or 2.5x speed. A thirty minute information video now only takes me about twelve minutes to watch. That saves a lot of hours for more productive activities over time.

You have to lock in and really focus on the content to still be able to learn it at that pace. I suggest only speeding it up by about 50% at first then slowly raising the speed as you get used to watching videos this way. It won't take long to get used to the increased pace. If you need to slow it down to take notes or review a point, there's typically a slider that will allow you to do that.

Because these kinds of software solutions change all the time, I've provided a link to whichever one is my current favorite along with all your other bonuses at www.findingfocusbook.com/resources

**Audios**

It's even easier to speed up consumption of audio material. Simply categorize the file as an Audiobook in iTunes or your favorite media player and you will have the option to speed up playback. If you're listening to a podcast, then the controls for speeding it up are right there in the app. If you've downloaded an audiobook through Audible or iTunes, then this functionality is included within the player itself as well.

This allows you to take a long book, lecture, or training that could normally require days of effort to consume, and compress all that information down to a few hours. You can listen to the audio at double or triple speed while taking a walk, traveling to work, or running errands. It's a great way to maximize your down time and engage in continuous learning.

**Written Words**

Newspapers, magazines, textbooks, and training manuals are not novels. Unless you're reading purely for pleasure, learn some basic speed reading techniques and cut the time you spend on this activity in half.

I love to read and wouldn't want to speed read though any of my favorite books, but most written words we consume on a daily basis don't fit into that category. Do you read books and magazines in the same fashion? Does the process go something like this: open it up, look at it, read and reread the same line or paragraph over and over without fully comprehending it, and then put it down when you get bored, tired, or distracted? If so, you're not alone. That's a pretty common experience. Instead, learn this one basic speed reading technique and scan through the material to extract the core concepts at a breakneck pace.

The basic concept behind speed reading is this: you are capable of visually extracting meaning from words a lot faster than you can verbally articulate them, but when most people read, they're actually saying those words in their mind and this slows down the process.

When you read, put your fingers to your lips and notice if the breath coming out is in an interrupted fashion. That would indicate that you are literally reading what it is that you're seeing. You could also put your finger on your Adam's apple to make the same determination. Your eyes may also tend to jump all around the page as you're reading, which reduces comprehension while increasing the time needed to consume it.

So here's a crash course in speed reading! Use your finger to trace a squiggly line down the page as you read. You'll only pick out certain key words when you do that. You don't really need to look at the edges of the lines, and you don't need to understand every single word in a given section of text in order to understand the meaning of it.

In fact, if you want to be really proactive about this, go grab a magazine right now. Select an article. Now just scan the first couple paragraphs of that article, scan the last couple of paragraphs, and determine if it's of interest and value before going back up through the subsections if necessary. If it is, then squiggle your finger down that center section and you will find that you've got the basic idea of what's written there without having to spend much time to discover it.

Start using your finger as a guide when you read printed materials. Don't worry about reading every word as though it were your favorite book. Just briefly scan through the text of most items that you read throughout the day. Squiggle your finger down the page and get the gist of it. In most cases, that's enough to get what you need to know without pulling your focus from more productive tasks.

## 9. Apply The 80/20 Rule

The 80/20 rule refers to an economic principle invented in the early 1900s by Italian economist Vilfredo Pareto. It was originally developed to explain wealth distribution but can be applied to pretty much every areas of our lives.

The concept goes like this: 80% of your results come from 20% of your efforts. 80% of your profits come from 20% of your investments. 80% of your problems come from 20% of your actions. And so on.

As applied to our core concept of focus, 80% of your effectiveness comes from 20% of your actions, so figure out what those most valuable activities are and focus on doing them as much as possible.

Do the reverse as well. Look at the 20% of your efforts which create the least valuable results, and stop doing them. Eliminate, delegate, or outsource all but your most valuable, meaningful, or gratifying tasks.

Instead of striving to be busy, decide to be effective. The less busy you are, the more effective you can become.

Being busy is just a by-product of indiscriminate thinking, inefficient actions, and a lack of priorities. You can uncover numerous ways to get more done with less effort by cutting out the 20% of your work that is the least valuable and focusing your efforts on the 20% that is the most valuable.

## 10. Eliminate, Delegate, & Outsource

You do not have to do everything yourself. Get used to outsourcing work that is time-consuming, undesirable, or outside your expertise. This applies to everything from hiring people to cut your lawn, clean your house, and change your oil to professional tasks that take up too much of your time. It may be more productive to delegate these activities to associates or outsource them to online virtual assistants in other countries for pennies on the dollar. It's an economic opportunity for them and an efficiency boon to you.

If your time is worth more than what it would cost to pay someone to do that work on your behalf, then there's no sense in doing it yourself. Of course, only outsource things that are outside of your expertise and enjoyment. Do that and you can free up a lot of extra time and energy to focus on what you love and do well so you can do more of it.

Determine how much your time is worth and then leverage it by only focusing on the most valuable work you do. If you're paid a salary, how much does that equate to per hour?

Start with your yearly take home pay or, if you're self-employed or an entrepreneur, average out your net income from the past three years to arrive at a realistic number.

Next, take your yearly net income and divide it by 50 for the typical working weeks of the year, and then divide that result by 40 for the number of hours in an average work week. That final number is how much you're earning on an hourly basis. Sure, you may work far more than 40 hours a week but we're just going after a ballpark number here for comparative purposes.

We can do the reverse calculation as well. If you're paid $10 an hour, multiply it by 40, that's $400 a week times 50 weeks which is $20,000 a year. If you're earning $20 an hour you're making $40,000 a year. If you make $50,000 a year you're earning $25 an hour, and so forth.

So determine how much it is that you make and back it out to determine how much that is per hour. Now look at all the tasks that you have to do this week and determine how much time they're likely to take you. If you can pay someone else to do those tasks for you more cheaply or efficiently than you can do them yourself, and get them done just as well or better, then that's exactly what you should do. This is called leveraging your time.

Take all your non-essential work – the things that take up 80% of your time and focus – and itemize them. Then see if you can simply eliminate the bottom 20%. If it's work that's not producing meaningful results, then why do it?

With the remaining 60%, find people to whom you can delegate or outsource. Surround yourself with good people who have complimentary skill sets. Then let them handle repetitive, low-value, and non-essential work so that you can focus on your top priorities.

If you can outsource it, use the internet to find people with specific specialties at reasonable rates. I currently use the following websites for this kind of work:

- www.odesk.com
- www.fiverr.com
- www.elance.com

On any given day, I've got several people working for me half way around the world while I sleep. My research assistant is in India, my transcriptionist is in the Philippines, and my graphic designer is in South Africa. They cost pennies on the dollar and since their local wages pay less than what we're used to here in the United States, it's a great deal for both parties.

You can outsource to people locally instead if you don't like the concept of the global economy. I also outsource to a neighborhood teenager who comes in once a week and does duplicating and various office tasks that are repetitive and time-consuming. I prefer to pay her $10 an hour to do this kind of work rather than have menial tasks consume my day.

I value my time much higher than $10 an hour, so it doesn't really make sense for me to spend half the day organizing and duplicating and mailing and cleaning and scanning when I can simply pay her a few bucks an hour to do so. You can do this, too.

This concept can be expanded beyond work to many areas of your life as well. For instance, I also hire local people to mow my lawn, change my oil, and wash my car. You can't do everything yourself and the more time you spend doing low-income producing work, the less time you'll have to achieve anything really meaningful.

If you've never delegated and outsourced before, then you may feel a bit of resistance to the idea. You may say to yourself, "But I'm not working right at this moment. I'm not getting paid anyway. These are my off hours so why should I pay somebody else to do things that I could do in my spare time?"

The simple truth of the matter is that the more you focus on doing low value work, the less time, energy, and focus you have for producing high value work. And when you're not working on high value tasks then it's more important to spend that free time improving your health and personal relationships instead of staying busy.

So write down all the low-value tasks you repeatedly do that can either be delegated, outsourced, or completely eliminated. Determine who the best person is to do those things – other than yourself. Then make the calls, send the emails, or schedule the meetings necessary to clear those tasks off your to-do list once and for all.

Leverage your time. Eliminate, delegate, and outsource. Focus instead on whatever creates the highest value.

# 11. Attain Inbox Zero

The more things you have in your inbox, the more things you have on your mind. Everything in your inbox represents a commitment of time and focus. But just because someone sends you an email doesn't mean they own a piece of your life. Multiply that email by the hundreds of emails most of us get each day and you have one of the greatest threats to focus and productivity that we face on a continuous basis.

It can literally waste hours of your day just going through emails and deleting or responding to them. If you do this before your three most important tasks, then you are unlikely to ever get meaningful work done.

Focus on clearing out your inbox for one hour. Time yourself and stick to that limit. Work fast and ruthlessly. Do one of three things with each email: trash it, file it for reference, or take action on it. Anything that requires longer than a minute to respond to, put in a separate "Action" folder. Any response that takes less than a minute, do as soon as you come across it. Again, this should take less than an hour. I don't care if you have hundreds of emails in your inbox.

Realize, too, that there are different ways of sorting your email, for instance, by date and by sender, so you'll first want to sort your emails by sender in order to go through this process quickly.

Your emails are probably listed based on the date that they arrived, but you can typically sort them by the name of the sender and group all of that person's messages together in a thread. If you haven't responded their inquiries in a while and you have 20 emails from them, just look at the most recent email from that person, respond to it, and then see if you can safely delete all the rest.

Go through that process, and if you still have time left over at the end of the hour, go through all your other email folders in the same manner. They tend to be the digital equivalent of shoe boxes in the attic. If you've not looked at them in at least a year, then delete or archive them. They're just gathering digital dust. Get them off of your email and out of your life. Play The Email Game to really speed up this process www.findingfocusbook. com/emailgame

### The Nuclear Option

Here's the quickest, easiest way to reach Inbox Zero and eliminate that focus draining backlog of emails.
Step 1: Select all of your emails
Step 2: Hit archive
Step 3: Focus on more meaningful activities

You know what will happen? People will email you about the important things again and the burden of going through everything else will be gone. I've done this several times in my own life. Just wiped the slate clean. It's scary until the moment you do it and then it's wonderful.

This is a big one. It's not going to take a lot of time, but it's going to take a big weight off of your shoulders. Commit to doing it. Remember, sort your emails by name first and this can be a surprisingly fast process. Put on some upbeat music and get to it!

## 12. Only Check Emails Twice A Day

Start responding to your emails twice a day and close your email client the rest of the time. I know they come in continuously and it seems important to answer them right when they arrive, but for the most part they're not that urgent and it doesn't really matter if you wait a few hours. It may matter if you wait a few days or a few weeks, but I'm only talking about a few hours.

Each time that you check your email and respond to them individually, it takes the focus off whatever higher-value task you were doing and introduces a distraction. It then takes time to refocus on whatever you were doing in the first place. Not just the time to respond to the email, it takes time to get back into gear to do productive things again once you've allowed yourself to become interrupted.

It might only take you a moment or two to respond to a given email, but it's also taken time and focus away from whatever you were doing in the first place and it's going to take time to get back into doing it again. If you start checking your email once in the morning and once in the late afternoon, you'll find no decrease in the quality of your communication, but a big increase in the amount of work you get done on a daily basis.

Oh, and don't check emails first thing in the morning or last thing at the end of the day. Check them after you do the most important thing on your post-it note in the morning, maybe an hour into your work schedule.

Open up your email client and answer, file, or delete everything that came in overnight. Then close it up again until later in the afternoon. If you've already cleared out your inbox that will be easy to do. Then, do the rest of your high-value work for the day and about an hour before you're done, check and respond to your emails again.

Close your email client or app when you're not using it and turn off push notifications. Don't allow people to destroy your focus throughout the day with those little Ding! Ding! Ding! sounds.

You're not Pavlov's dog salivating at the sound of the bell. You have the freedom to turn that bell off. Do it and reclaim your ability to focus on email at the times you determine, not when some random email sender wants your attention. Schedule email interactions twice a day and that's it. Do it for a week and you'll be hooked.

## 13. Only Touch Papers Once

Sitting down at your desk to get work done while there's a pile of papers on it is like trying to swim through a sea of spaghetti. You can do it, but there's so much coming at you that just making the attempt can seem overwhelming.

Only touch papers once, and sort them into three piles to take the next action. All the papers that you have in your life can either be trashed, scanned for later reference, or immediately attended to. So take any papers that you have in front of you right now, pick up one piece of paper and ask yourself, "Is there any action that I can take on this right now?"

Does it necessitate a phone call, a bill payment, an email? Whatever it is, define what that is and do it. If you can't take action on it right now, then either scan it or trash it. Do that with each piece of paper until there are no pieces of paper left on your desk. This is exactly like reaching inbox zero.

**Dropbox vs Evernote**

You can scan all of the paper on your desk into either Dropbox or Evernote. But which one is better? That depends on how your mind works. I personally use Dropbox but lots of people swear by Evernote.

Dropbox is like a digital filling cabinet, so if your mind likes to sort through things in that kind of closed architecture, then Dropbox is the best option for you. I like thinking of my digital documents as being in files within drawers within cabinets. That makes sense to me, so I love the way Dropbox is structured.

If you prefer a more open architecture, then you can use Evernote. That's more like a never ending pile of post-its and notepads. The great thing about Evernote is that all of the content in those scanned documents is instantly searchable so you can look through those piles of PDFs quickly and easily.

You may want to use both Dropbox and Evernote for different purposes. Just don't leave all those papers lying around. Every time you look at them, shuffle and readjust their positioning, it drains focus from more important tasks.

There's no reason to have a desk cluttered with papers when these free tools exist and are just a click away.

## 14. Chunk Big Projects Down To Size

It can seem difficult to take action on larger projects when you don't know where to begin. But if you break the project down into its component parts and then list the actionable steps you can take on each one of those subsections, then the whole endeavor becomes much more manageable.

This is a technique known as 'chunking'.

Once you've done that, it's important to take at least one of those actionable steps every day so as to create consistent momentum. Eventually all those little steps will add up to a marathon's worth of progress.

It's taken me months to write this book. How did I do it? One day at a time. If I had started the process by thinking, "I need to write 30,000 words that are worth reading," then it would seem so overwhelming that I'd be like a deer in the headlights, just staring at the glow from the screen, unable to do anything at all.

The secret to writing a book or accomplishing any big project is the same:

1. Define the specific outcome you wish to accomplish
2. Reverse engineer the specific actions you'll need to take to get from here to there and break them down into bite sized "chunks"
3. Then consistently focus on taking the next step, one step at a time, until you've taken every step

Put one foot in front of the other on a predetermined path, do that every day, and before you know it you will have reached your destination.

## 15. Ten Minutes Early Is On Time

On time is not on time, on time is late. 10 minutes early is on time.

How many times have you found yourself rushing to get to an appointment because you thought you were going to be late? Grabbing your things and running out the door, trying to get your thoughts and things in order, arriving at your destination just barely in time? Then you're not able to focus at the meeting itself because you're stressed out from the ordeal you just went through to get there!

Start making it your mission to arrive at your appointments at least 10 minutes early. Don't try to trick yourself by setting your watch to the wrong time either – your subconscious will catch on and you'll still be late. Just decide that it's easier to focus when you're early and make the effort to do it consistently. It's also more respectful of the other person's time.

You want to find better focus? Then start getting where you need to go earlier. It will give you a few moments in order to catch your breath, organize your thoughts, and focus on your objectives.

An appointment is a commitment to show up. Being on time is a way of being true to your word. It's important. Ten minutes early is on time.

## 16. Minimize Clutter

Do you own your things or do your things own you? Well I think the answer is pretty obvious. Our things own us. Our things require not only an investment of money to purchase them initially, but an investment of focus in order to keep them like new.

Most of us have our lives filled with things we don't use or don't need. Get rid of what you don't need or use so you can better focus on what remains.

If there are clothes in your closet that you haven't worn in over two years, then chances are you probably won't wear them in the next two years either. Put them in a bag and give them away to someone in need.

Take everything out of your desk and so the same thing. If you're not going to use it, constantly moving it out of the way to find what you do need is a drain on your focus that can easily be eliminated.

Go through everything in your desk, in your office, and eventually in your life with two bins – one, fill with things to throw out; another, fill with things to either give away or post on Craigslist or eBay.

If you give things away, see if you can give them directly to a person in need. Direct giving is most effective for the recipient and most gratifying for you.

If you're going to post things on Craigslist or eBay, make sure it's worth your time to do it. I don't understand why people post things that are worth less than $10 when it's going to take you time and energy to post it, respond to people's inquiries, package it, and mail it. If you're making less than $10 an hour perhaps that's worthwhile. If you're making more than $10 an hour, then it's a poor use of your time. So if any individual item is worth less than a few bucks, either throw it out or give it to someone who can make better use of it than you.

Once you complete this process and get what you don't need out of your life, it will increase your focus immeasurably. Honestly, it's one of my favorite things to do.

People joke about "retail therapy" – shopping to feel better about themselves – but acquiring more things simply can't compare to eliminating unnecessary things. It's like pruning an unwieldy bush into a beautiful bonsai. What remains is a thing of beauty worthy of your focus and attention.

## 17. Be A Perfecting-ist

Be a Perfecting-ist not a Perfectionist. There is nothing made by you or I that is perfect – because people are imperfect. We are all flawed and therefore so is our work. Perfection is the realm of nature not man.

When we work on things until they're perfect, we find that day never comes and we rob the world of our output. Certainly, it is important to do the best work you're capable of producing, but be continually in the process of perfecting rather than making perfect so you can continue producing.

Perfectionism kills productivity. Perfecting-ism produces quality work.

## 18. Don't Multitask

Focus on the present moment because it's really all we have anyway. As Master Oogway said in that timeless philosophical treatise known as *Kung Fu Panda*, "Yesterday is history, tomorrow is a mystery, but today is a gift. That is why it is called the present." Sure he's an animated turtle, but he's right.

One of the strange things about being human is that we have the capability of multitasking ourselves right out of our very existences. How much time have you spent rehashing things that happened in the past, about which you can no longer do anything at all, or thinking about what may or may not come to pass in the future, and completely missing the present moment? The present is really all we have.

All it takes is the awareness that all we have is the present and the resolution to not multitask – to give as much value as possible to whatever it is we are doing at the moment, and to whomever is in front of us.

Make it your mission to give value to whomever is in front of you and to focus as fully as possible on whatever you're doing in the present moment. You'll get more gratification out of everything you do, and you'll find that you do things better and faster as well.

## 19. Use This Daily Action Plan

Commit to following this action plan every day as a way of systemizing your progress toward becoming more focused and productive.

I've provided this form for you as a free download so you can print it out and fill it out every day.

Get it at www.findingfocusbook.com/action

**DAILY ACTION PLAN**

**Self-Esteem:** Do The Mirror Exercise (and really mean it)

**Mental / Emotional:** Today I am grateful for (list 5 things)

_____

_____

_____

_____

_____

**Social:** I will limit my social media time to _____ minutes

**Physical:** I will do the following good things for my body today...

- Drink water (no other drinks)
- Eat no sugar (naturally occurring sugar, such as in whole fruit, is fine)
- Walk at least 10,000 steps

**Extra Credit:** Listen to the relaxation meditation audio at www.findingfocusbook.com/meditation breathe deeply, and focus internally on living in the present moment, letting go of what you cannot change, and creating greater value in your life and the lives of others.

## 20. Take Responsibility

A lot of time and energy can be wasted focusing blame on people and circumstances for where we are in our lives. You can achieve far more by forgiving them, forgiving yourself, being grateful for all that you can, and taking responsibility for everything in your life.

Commit to improving who you are and what you do every single day and you will find your way to where you want to be. It's not so much an action you take as a decision you make. Here's an exercise you can do right now to help reinforce that decision.

### Self Acceptance Exercise

Take a nice deep breath and just relax.

Notice the quality of your breath and be at peace with yourself and your environment as you turn your focus inward.

Say to yourself:

"I am the result of all my past thinking up until now."

Take another deep breath and accept the truth of that statement.

Now say to yourself:

"I take full responsibility for everything in my life."

And as you release that breath realize how empowering that statement is.

Finally, say to yourself:

"Every day in every way I'm becoming better and better."
And believe it, because it's true.

## 21. Focus On Time Freedom

Once you've implemented the preceding tips you'll work in a much more focused fashion. That will produce more and better results from your efforts. And what will you get in return for generating all that added value? The potential for more profit and more free time.

More money is great, up to a point, but eventually you'll have everything you want and all there is left for you to do is give it away. When it comes to time however, we can never have enough because it's a non-renewable resource. Unlike money, once it's spent you can never make more of it. So as you get better about focus in your work, remember to balance that out by enjoying all the additional free time that increased productivity creates.

Imagine what you would do if you had an extra 2 hours free today and every day of your life. Where would you go, what would you do, and who would you do it with. Reconnect with the reason you're doing this in the first place.

Finding focus allows you to do more in less time so you can enjoy the time freedom that creates. As the pressure lifts and your productivity rises, remember to enjoy all the freedom that gives you. Reward yourself for a job well done and appreciate your own accomplishments by balancing your work with play. Time freedom is your reward for working with focus. Enjoy it :-)

# 14

# Become More Decisive

*"Don't just do something, stand there"*
**– The White Rabbit, *Alice in Wonderland***

At the time of this writing, my son wears the same thing to preschool each and every day. Black pants, electric guitar underwear, a blue collared shirt with a picture of a guitar on it, and a blue striped fedora. He calls this his "Rock Star" outfit and, because he insists on wearing it every single day, we have several of them. Before that, he wore a Batman outfit (right down to the Batman underwear) every day for about a year. We had several of those outfits, too.

Rather than fight his impulse to wear the same thing every day, I celebrate it – because it puts him in the company of great thinkers like Steve Jobs and Einstein.

The point of telling you this is not to convince you to wear the same thing every day but to point out why that's actually a very beneficial idea. It helps to eliminate "decision fatigue" which is a concept that's been gaining traction in recent years as productivity suffers under the weight of information overload.

It's estimated that in any given day we have about 100 opportunities to make good, well-reasoned decisions and then after that point the stress of making them begins to set in and we begin to react to things emotionally rather than logically. That's why car dealers offer you undercoating and extras at the end of the process, when you're worn out and offer less resistance.

If you use up too much of your decision-making capacity early in the day on such minor details as deciding what clothes you're going to wear, what you're going to eat for breakfast, and so on, then you're setting the tone for the rest of the day in a way that's not conclusive to maximum creativity and effectiveness.

If you instead conserve those energies for when you can really make an impact through your decisions and systemize your mornings into a predictable routine, it will introduce an element of calm and control that will set you on a path toward greater decisiveness when it counts.

Decisiveness is crucial to working well under pressure. Many times just making a decision, any decision, is preferable to inaction. Unfortunately, as decision fatigue sets in, it becomes harder to make well-reasoned decisions and your results suffer.

In a *New York Times* Magazine article on this topic, science columnist John Tierney reports that researchers studied 1,100 Israeli judicial decisions over the course of a year and found that, "Prisoners who appeared early in the morning received parole about 70 percent of the time, while those who appeared late in the day were paroled less than 10 percent of the time. ...The mental work of ruling on case after case, whatever the individual merits, wore them down."

The more choices you make through the day the harder it will be to muster the mental energy to continue making them well.

Therefore, seek to minimize your minor decisions so as to achieve maximum effectiveness for your major decisions.

You can accomplish this goal by making a morning checklist in advance, laying out your clothes the night before, and always eating the same thing for breakfast.

Or you can wear the same clothes every day, have someone else cook your meals, and get driven around by your own personal chauffeur as my son does, lucky little kid that he is :-)

# Morning Systemization Exercise

Determine three things that you can do tomorrow morning to systemize the process. Plan them out tonight and eliminate those decisions from your morning routine.

1. Tomorrow morning I will eat

_____

2. Tomorrow I will wear

_____

3. Tomorrow I will do (list the 3 most important things)

_____

_____

_____

_____

_____

_____

_____

_____

_____

# 15

# Reduce Exposure:
## Email, Social Media, TV

*"Great minds discuss ideas; average minds discuss
events; small minds discuss people"*
– Eleanor Roosevelt

## Email

To reduce your exposure, close your email when you don't need it.
Having it open all the time is a distraction and leads to information
overload. How many times a day does this happen: you're in the
middle of a project, you're being productive, and DING! – your
email goes off and you stop what you're doing to see what it is. It's
a completely Pavlovian response and it takes time to regain your
focus after that interruption.

So you answer that email, go back to what you were doing,
take a few minutes to get back on track, and DING! – you get
interrupted again. When that happens over and over throughout
the day, it drains all the focus from your work.

And don't tell me, "Oh, that's not a problem because I multitask really well." Multitasking is a fallacy. When we attempt to
multitask, we don't do anything well. We can only do one thing
at a time so what people think of as multitasking is actually just
rapidly switching focus back and forth. And that hurts both the
quality and the quantity of your output.

Usually that email can wait. It can wait at least an hour or
until you're done with the task at hand. If it's really urgent, they're
going to text you, they're going to call you, they're going to keep

emailing you or you're going to find out when you open the email in an hour anyway. When you keep your email client open all the time, it constantly calls to you for attention and it can be hard to resist. That decreases productivity and increases stress.

Instead, see if you can just close your email program during work periods and open it only at predetermined times, like once in the morning, once before lunch, once after lunch, and once at the end of the day? Believe me, that's more than enough email interactions to respond to people in a timely fashion without getting constantly interrupted throughout the day.

## Social Media

Everything I just said about email applies even more so to social media. That Twitter feed and Facebook news feed are endless distractions. Simply close them and only open them back up again as a reward when you complete whatever you're working on.

I'm on Facebook nearly every day. It's a great way to keep in touch with family and friends. I even have private Facebook groups set up to support people who do my online and group coaching programs. But I don't keep Facebook open on my laptop and phone all the time. I schedule social media time as a fifteen minute reward break a few times a day. Just like email, closing it until predetermined times makes all the difference to your focus and productivity.

Two or three times a day, after I've completed all my calls or reacquired inbox zero or finished paperwork, I'll open Facebook and enjoy the experience without apology. And then I'll close it. That may be hard to do at first if you're used to being on there all the time. If you don't, though, then it has the potential to pull you away from more meaningful interactions, like actually talking to the person sitting across from you at the dinner table!

According to a Boston University study published on *Computers In Human Behavior*, researchers have found that heavy social media use is "a positive, significant predictor of divorce rate and spousal troubles". Specifically, heavy social media users have been found to be 32% more likely to think about leaving their spouse.

Now, certainly that's not the same as saying they actually acted on those thoughts, but is it any wonder? The next time you're at a restaurant, look around at all the couples who are connecting on social media instead of with one another. They're giving more importance to their virtual relationships than their real ones, so it's only a matter of time until the quality of their real relationships becomes virtually nonexistent.

## Working With Timed Intervals

It's also important to physically close your social media apps and web pages after a timed interval, like 10 or 15 minutes, and stick to that. Don't get sucked out of your life and into their virtual reality. That's when it becomes a time vampire and a relationship killer.

You can use a Pomodoro app, as discussed in the productivity section, to set up timed intervals for work and play while you're at your desk. Believe me, even though you'll be scheduling in periods of social media decompression, it will increase your overall productivity so much the rest of the time that it will more than make up for those breaks.

## TV and the News

During the first twenty minutes of the day and the last twenty minutes of the day you're very responsive to suggestion. You're in Theta brain wave state which is what occurs when you're having a lucid dream.

When you're at that point and you're just waking up in the morning or you're just going to sleep at night, whatever messages you're exposed to and which affect you emotionally take hold in your subconscious mind. They can have undue influence on you and can change the course of your day or your night. A better choice is to focus on improving yourself during those naturally hypnotic moments at the start and end of every day.

But what do most people do? Watch and listen to the news. And what's broadcast as news? Negative, emotionally-charged images, events, and talking heads filling your consciousness with things you wish you could change but are powerless to do anything about.

Remember our definition of what causes stress? *Something you want to change but are powerless to do anything about.* Where else is that more clearly demonstrated than on the news?

"If it bleeds it leads" is a common refrain in the news business. Far from seeking to inform and educate its viewers, the news, as it exists in our society today, is a constant source of fear, paranoia, anger, and worry.

Many wonderful things happen in the world every day and some terrible things, too. But if you watch the news you would think that scenario was reversed – that the world is a scary place always about to erupt with violence and disease everywhere you look.

Don't look now, but your babysitter could be planning on kidnapping your kids! That food in your refrigerator just might kill you! Or the current popular favorite – true crime reenactments so salacious as to be referred to as "murder porn". They're the most popular programming segments on certain cable news networks and have been for years.

The point is, willingly exposing yourself to the news is like having risky sex. It might feel stimulating for the moment, but you're left with a mind full of worry and fear that you can do nothing about. It creates a lot of noise and distraction in our society and can become emotionally debilitating.

Harvard researchers have even found that this kind of prolonged exposure to anxiety producing stimulus destroys "telomeres", which are chromosomal proteins that regulate the aging process.

Watching the news causes an emotional response that literally ends up prematurely aging you through worry and fear! It's not worth it. The price you pay for exposing yourself to all that negative noise is far too great.

You can't do anything to change what's happening half way around the world. And if you see those violent images of people getting shot, car crashes, home invasions, and talking heads yelling at each other enough, it's only a matter of time until that anger and fear gets inside of you. The world will start to seem like a very scary place.

When you put that in your brain and your body and your emotions the first thing in the morning and last thing at night, it elevates your stress level. No wonder a third of the population has sleep issues – they're putting nightmare scenarios into their minds right before they go to sleep!

Turn it off.

Believe me, you will still know what's going on. It's in the zeitgeist. You will know when an election is coming up. When something monumental is happening, people will be talking about it or it will pop up on your phone. Someone will tell you about it. You will not become ignorant, only more efficient and emotionally balanced. All the day-to-day violence and distress will recede from your focus and you will be better able to live in the present moment and stay true to the reality of your own life.

Let go of the things that you are powerless to change, such as just about everything in the news. It's meant to upset you. That's how they get eyeballs. That's how they get viewership – by agitating you, not informing you. So turn it off, especially first thing in the morning and last thing at night. Focus on appreciating all that you have to be grateful for in life instead.

You'll be amazed at how powerful an action that is. How pervasively it can affect your emotions and the way you see the world around you. Think of how much more time you'll have reclaimed as your own and how much more positive your focus will be, instead of feeling like everyone is out to get you and your children and that the world is going to hell in a hand basket.

And while you're at it, limit your exposure to TV in general. Treat it the same way I've suggested you interact with social media, as a reward limited to timed intervals. Not as background noise that's sapping your focus throughout the day.

Statistically, the higher your income and education the less TV you'll watch. According to the latest Neilson data people with four years of college or more watch an average of an hour and 14 minutes of prime time, versus those with just a high school education, who watch two hours and eight minutes. Income levels correspond in similar ways – Daytime viewing equates to an hour and 12 minutes for those making $100,000 or more, versus an hour and 58 minutes for those making $30,000 or less.

Which group do you want to belong to? Model the behaviors of successful people and you will move into closer alignment with that success yourself.

Limited email, social media, and TV viewing to timed intervals instead of constant background noise and you will certainly become more productive and less stressed as a result. At the very least, you won't feel so overwhelmed with things to do and will have a lot more free time.

# PART 4

## FOCUS ON YOUR SUCCESS

# 16

# The Meaning of Success

*"Try not to become a person of success,*
*but rather try to become a person of value"* – **Albert Einstein**

Let's focus on WHY we're doing all this for a moment. It's important to be process oriented, but you can't chart your journey if you haven't picked a destination.

Once you're able to find focus whenever you need it, minimize distractions, and work well under pressure then what? How will you know when you're successful? And what is "success" anyway?

Most people define success in monetary terms – earning a certain amount or having a certain amount in assets. Becoming a millionaire used to be thought of as having achieved success, but a million doesn't really get you all that far these days, does it? So do you need to have two million now to be considered successful? More?

Or is it income-based? Does a six figure income make you successful? Then again, it's not what you make, it's what you keep.

Or is it what you drive? A luxury car, a Louis Vuitton handbag, or a Rolex watch: they all exist to communicate to others that you are successful. And a lot of people certainly buy into that notion.

The problem with defining your success in terms of monetary wealth or physical possessions, of course, is that it's all transient and ephemeral. It's not you. You are not your Bugatti or your Rolex. You are not your bank account. If the stock market crashes and your investments lose half their value, that doesn't mean you lose half your value. You may be worth less on paper, but you're not worth less as a human being. Unless you buy into the idea that success is measured externally.

My favorite definition of success comes from the 1950's Earl Nightingale recording, "The Strangest Secret".

*"Success is the progressive realization of a worthy goal or ideal."*

Now there's an empowering idea!

When you wake up every day excited about what you can accomplish that will move you a little bit closer toward your goals, then the work itself becomes its own reward. Success becomes about creating value, not acquiring things.

I can tell you from experience that the saying, "Do what you love and you'll never work a day in your life" is true. It's not that you don't work when you love what you do – you actually work harder because you love doing it – it's just that the work feels joyful and rewarding.

You don't have to quit your job to have this experience either. Find what you love about what you do and focus on that aspect of your work. Then tie it to progressively realized accomplishments that you can work toward on a daily basis and you've got a real formula for self-determined success.

Passionately work toward achieving your goals and ideals, creating value in your life and the lives of others every day, and you will be successful... by definition.

## The Fisherman Story

I first encountered this parable in the writings of the Brazilian lyricist and novelist, Paulo Coelho, who describes it as a classic story present in many cultures. Tim Ferriss also included a version of it in his excellent book "The 4-Hour Workweek". I'm sharing it with you here because I think it gets to the heart of what success really is.

What do you really want? Why do you want it? How are you going to get it? And how will you know when you have it?

You can claim your own success right now if you can answer those questions and are committed to living your life progressively realizing those ideals.

## The Fisherman and The Businessman

A successful businessman took a well-deserved vacation to a quaint little coastal fishing village in Brazil. As he stood on the pier, looking out at the sea, he watched a small boat with just one young Brazilian fisherman pull into the dock. Inside the fishing boat were several large yellowfin tuna. A good catch, as the contented smile on the fisherman's face made clear.

The American complimented the Brazilian on the quality of his fish. "How long did it take you to catch them?" he asked.

"Oh, just a few hours," the fisherman replied.

The businessman wondered aloud, "Then why don't you stay out longer and catch more fish?"

The fisherman said, "With this I have more than enough to support my family and provide for their needs."

"But what do you do with the rest of your time?" asked the businessman, genuinely mystified at his lack of drive and ambition.

Smiling, the fisherman answered, "I sleep late, fish a little, play with my children, take a nap with my wife, stroll into the village each evening where I sip wine, sing a few songs, and play guitar with my friends."

The businessman shook his head at the thought of all that lost opportunity. "Look, I have an MBA and I can help you to become more profitable. Here's what you do. Start by fishing several hours longer, every day. Then sell the extra fish you catch and with the additional proceeds you can buy a bigger boat. That larger boat will in turn bring in more money and then before long you can buy a second boat, then a third, and so on, until you have an entire fleet of fishing boats."

The fisherman's eyes opened wide. "That would bring in a lot more fish.'

"Exactly!" exclaimed the businessman, happy that the fisherman was starting to see the light. "Then, instead of selling your catch to a middleman, you'll be able to sell your fish directly to the processor, or even open your own cannery. Eventually, you could control the product, processing, and distribution. You could leave this tiny coastal village and move to the city, or even Los Angeles or New York, where you'd run the headquarters of your expanding enterprise."

Having never thought of such things before in his life, the simple fisherman asked, "But how long will all this take?"

To which the businessman replied, "About 15 to 20 years. Less if you work really hard."

"But what do I do then?" asked the fisherman.

The businessman laughed and said, "Why that's the best part. When the time is right you would announce an IPO and sell your company stock to the public and become very rich. You would make millions!"

"Millions? Really? What would I do with it all?" asked the young fisherman in disbelief.

The businessman thrust out his arms and proudly proclaimed, "Then you could happily retire with all the money you've made! You could move to a quaint coastal fishing village where you could sleep late, play with your grandchildren, take naps with your wife, and stroll into the village in the evenings to sip wine, play the guitar and sing with your friends."

**The Moral:** When you know what you want, why you're working in the first place, and can identify when you've got it, then success becomes a daily reality and the work itself becomes its own reward.

# 17

# Improve Response:
## Gratitude & Physiology

*"When you arise in the morning, think of what a precious privilege
it is to be alive – to breathe, to think, to enjoy, to love"*
– Marcus Aurelius

## Attitude of Gratitude

In the previous section I recommended turning off the news because it creates worry and fear. So what's the opposite emotional experience that we can cultivate instead? The easy answer is courage – but courage is characterized by action whereas worry and fear are characterized as an emotional state.

The actual opposite of worry and fear is inner peace and love. I know, "Kumbaya," right? It may sound hippy-dippy but the absolute best way to improve your response to stress, pressure, and overwhelm is to cultivate an awareness of inner-peace and love. And here's a simple way to do that:

Spend a few minutes every day focusing on all the things for which you're grateful. Add new ones every day. Eventually, find a way to be grateful for everything.

Cultivating an attitude of gratitude can have the exact opposite effect as watching the news. Thinking about, talking about, and writing about all the things for which you are grateful and then sharing that with others actually lowers cortisol (the stress hormone).

Memory, decision-making, and critical thinking all become easier when focusing on what's good in your life. It makes you a more effective person when you tune out the noise of negative distractions and focus instead on what's good and positive and all that you can be thankful for.

You can still be a realist (if that's your disposition, as it is mine), but be an optimistic realist who is wise enough to follow the advice in the old Johnny Mercer song: "accentuate the positive, eliminate the negative, latch on to the affirmative, and don't mess with Mister In-Between".

If you believe you are deserving of good things, if you believe that the things in your life are beneficial to you and the people in your life have your best interests at heart, then when new events and experiences come your way, they will be filtered through that perspective.

If you believe the opposite, they will be filtered accordingly. Your expectations inform your actions and reactions. So transform your expectation to appreciation. Imagine every person was put in front of you so they can help you, you can help them, and you both can help each other.

Every experience is a new opportunity for growth. Be grateful to be the person you are, with the experiences you've had, and the opportunities unfolding before you.

Get in the habit of having an attitude of gratitude. You'll feel an enhanced sense of well-being and so will the other people with whom you're communicating.

What's the worst that's going to happen? Every once in a while someone will take advantage of your generous nature. It happens to all of us at some point. Learn what lessons you can from the experience and let them go. Move on, move past them, and don't let them bring you down.

You deserve better in your life so go out and find it. Demand it. Be the best and highest version of yourself and eventually you will fill your life with people who value who you are and what you have to offer.

Don't settle. Project an attitude of gratitude in all that you do and seek to find the good in every situation.

## The Story of The King and The Cannibal

A long time ago, in a far away land, there was a king. And this king had a close friend who had the habit of saying "this is good" about everything that happened in life no matter what it was. This always annoyed the king, but he let it go because they were friends.

One day the king and his friend were out hunting. The king's friend loaded a gun and handed it to the king, but he loaded it the wrong way and when the king fired it, his thumb was blown off.

"This is good!" exclaimed his friend.

The horrified and bleeding king was furious. "How can you say this is good? This is obviously horrible!" he shouted.

The king put his friend in jail.

About a year later the king went hunting by himself. Cannibals captured him and took him to their village. They tied his hands, stacked some wood, set up a stake and bound him to it. As they came near to set fire to the wood, they noticed that the king was missing a thumb. Being superstitious, they never ate anyone who was less than whole. They untied the king and sent him on his way.

Full of remorse, the king rushed to the prison to release his friend. "You were right, it WAS good," the king said.

The king told his friend how the missing thumb saved his life and added, "I feel so sad that I locked you in jail. That was such a bad thing to do."

"NO! This is good!" responded his delighted friend.

"Oh, how could that be good, my friend? I did a terrible thing to you and I owe you my life."

"It is good," said his friend, "because if I wasn't in jail I would have been hunting with you and they would have killed ME."

## Posture And Your Physiology

You can project success and actually change your own perception of how successful you are simply by adopting the posture of successful people. The reverse is also true.

Adopt a negative posture for a moment. Cross everything. Cross your arms, your legs, bend your head down, angle everything. It doesn't feel very empowering does it?

This is negative body language. You are bracing yourself against something or barricading yourself against something.

Now try an open posture. Go ahead and shake it out first. Now sit forward a little bit in your chair. Feet flat on the floor. Hands in your lap. Roll your shoulders back. Imagine there's an invisible string on the top of your head, lifting your head up and slightly out. Like what ballet dancers do for their get-ready pose.

Don't force it, don't strain. Just lift and elongate your spine. Breathe slowly and deeply, in through your nose and out through your mouth. Feels good, right? A strong open posture and deep measured breath communicates very positive body language and opens you up to better social interactions.

Now, let's go all the way and adopt power poses. Stand up and strike your favorite super hero pose. Wide stance, hands on hips, master of the universe. Or sit down, lean back, hands clasped behind your head, expansive posture like you own the place.

Nonverbal communication is demonstrated though body language. It creates judgments and influences attitudes that determine the quality of all kinds of social interactions and the way people feel about you. This is fairly well-known.

What's less well-known and even more important is that it influences the way you feel about yourself.

Social scientist Amy Cuddy, in her popular TED talk on body language, poses the question, "Do our nonverbals govern how we think and feel about ourselves?" And the answer is, "Absolutely YES!

Our minds can change our bodies and, as it turns out, it's equally true that our bodies can change our minds. Adopting power poses (such as the confident stances of super heroes) has been shown to raise testosterone and lower cortisol in as little as two minutes.

Cuddy and her team at Harvard studied what happens when you assume high power poses or low power poses for two minutes. They ran the experiment, took measurements before and after, and these were the results:

- Risk tolerance went from 60% to 86%.
- From the baseline starting point, the high power posers had a 25% decrease in their cortisol levels and low power posers had a 10% increase.
- Testosterone had a 30% differential between high power and low power poses. And remember, this all happened in just 2 minutes.

Assuming high power postural poses changes your self-talk, your hormones, and your emotional state. It allows you to feel more passion, presence, comfort, authenticity, confidence, and enthusiasm. It also projects an feeling of success both to others and yourself.

As a speaker and entertainer, I know this to be true. I have a backstage ritual I go through in the last few seconds before I take the stage where I jump up and down and punch the air like a prize fighter. It fills my body with oxygen and adrenaline and quickly focuses my energy on making a massive impact.

I don't care how weird it may look to the backstage crew, it works. I become that person who is going to conquer any obstacle. My body convinces my mind that success is imminent and that influences my behavior to create that outcome. You can do this, too. It's as easy as standing and moving with power.

## Power Pose Exercise

Spend two minutes doing power poses before your next social interaction and then notice how that changes the way you approach the situation. Notice how it affects other people's response to you as well.

# 18

# Minimize To Self Actualize

*"He is richest who is content with the least,*
*for content is the wealth of nature"* – **Socrates**

When people put the focus of their happiness on the outside, it leads to the acquisition of things as markers for success. They do things so they can have things so they can be somebody. Do. Have. Be.

This creates behaviors that are outcome-oriented rather than process-oriented. Forcing yourself to work on something because there is a paycheck in it and you need that money to buy something (or pay for something you've already bought) does not produce the best possible performance. It produces stress, resentment, and a feeling of having to work rather than a passionate desire to contribute.

This process can lead to an endless cycle of acquiring things to feel pleasure but then being required to work to pay for it. It ends up feeling like a trap and that's because it is.

With the exception of your basic human needs (food, water, shelter, clothing, and love), accumulating things in order to feel fulfilled, to "be", is disempowering and stress-producing. Ultimately, this leads not to happiness and contentment but to debt and a form of indentured servitude to the things that you possess. Debt is a form of slavery, after all, so if you're working to pay for things, then those things end up owning you – not the other way around.

Certainly we all like to have some possessions in this world. I'm not suggesting you forsake all your worldly goods or anything. In my own life, I have one too many cars. I keep a convertible in the driveway that I've had since my early 20s because I enjoy looking at it and it reminds me of my youth even though I rarely drive it because there is no back seat for my two small children.

Is this a contradiction? A double standard? Not really, because that convertible was paid for long ago and doesn't influence what I do on any given day unless it's to take a break and drive up the beach with the top down and the wind in my hair (what's left of it!).

Logically, I should get rid of that car. It's an unnecessary possession that I have to take care of to maintain in good working condition. Emotionally, I enjoy having it and it doesn't define who I am or what I do.

But there was a time when I owned so many things that they filled up two entire houses! I just kept accumulating things I rarely used and they all had to be put somewhere. Come to think of it, I also had a storage unit around that time. Sheesh.

Storage units are where possessions go to die when you just can't bear to get rid of them yet. Garages can become like storage units in that way. So can basements and attics. All these "things" weigh a person down. They become baggage that you carry with you throughout your life. That produces background stress. Believe me, it does, more than you may realize.

When you minimize your positions it allows you to focus on just those things that are truly worth having. And when you eliminate everything else, it alleviates the burden of having to be responsible for maintaining, storing, and owning them. It's a very freeing thing to do.

## Decluttering Exercise

Take a look around in your own life. What do you own that's weighing you down, causing you stress, and not adding to your sense of happiness and well-being. Can you get rid of it? Sell it or give it to someone who will benefit from it more? If so, then do that.

Assess all your possessions this way. Do they add to or detract from your life? Does having them increase or decrease your stress levels? Would you be better off without it? If so, then do something about it!

Most of us are drowning in our possessions. We have more than enough but keep working to acquire even more than we already have. There is a more gratifying way to live and all it takes is reversing the order of a few words. Instead of Do, Have, Be what if you Be, Have, Do?

In other words, instead of working to buy things to feel more significant or better about yourself, what if that feeling of significance and satisfaction came from within? Then your acquisitions would support who you are rather than define you. And your actions, at work and elsewhere, would emanate from a place of centered well-being rather than need. A desire to create and give back rather than the need to get a paycheck.

Be. Have. Do.

That's a sequence that leads to a lean, uncluttered, focused, passionate life.

I'm proud to say that today I've downsized my possessions to one modest little house filled with light and children rather than piles and boxes and stacks of things.

It's much easier to focus on what's important in your life when you get rid of all the things that are blocking your vision. Minimize to self-actualize.

# 19

# How To Make Your Own Luck

*"The best luck of all is the luck you make for yourself"*
– Douglas MacArthur

The lottery. Most people say, "You can't win if you don't play". But I say, "It's the playing that's keeping you from winning." The reason I've never bought a lottery ticket in my life is because I don't want to program my mind to believe that success is unpredictable. When you think the way to riches is through a random act like winning the lottery, then it saps your motivation to achieve through the value of your own work.

It gets down to your belief about whether luck happens to you or because of you. Do you believe you make your own luck or do you believe it falls from the sky, raining good or bad down upon your head depending on the mysterious whims of fate?

More than hard work, talent, or intelligence, luck can determine your ultimate level of success. A chance meeting, an unexpected opportunity, or the exact moment you cross a busy intersection can have a profound effect upon your life.

When reading "the exact moment you cross a busy intersection", what image comes to your mind? Getting hit by a car? Or just missing getting hit by a car?

Your answer to that question reveals a lot about the thoughts and behaviors responsible for what people refer to as luck.

Researchers at UCLA and Columbia University studied the

psychology of luck. They found that our beliefs about luck can be divided into two categories: stable or fleeting.

People who think that luck is stable, a fairly constant phenomenon, believe that people are generally either lucky or unlucky. That they themselves either have good luck or bad luck.

People who think of luck as fleeting, believe that it's unpredictable and capricious. Good luck and bad luck happen to them – not because of them.

Their findings go on to demonstrate that people's beliefs about luck impact their drive for success, because people who think of their luck as stable have a higher drive in the face of adversity. They put the locus of control within themselves.

People who believe in luck as transitory (fleeting) are more prone to superstition. They put the locus of control outside of themselves. That belief is disempowering and not in your own best interest.

Also, superstitions don't work. They are random and ineffectual, giving only the illusion of control. In some cultures black cats are considered bad luck and in others they are considered good luck. In point of fact, they are neither. They are just cats.

Dr Richard Wiseman, author of the book, *The Luck Factor*, conducted a 10-year study on luck with hundreds of people and documented the results. As a result, he identified the four principles that determine good fortune.

Lucky people "are skilled at creating and noticing chance opportunities, make lucky decisions by listening to their intuition, create self-fulfilling prophesies via positive expectations, and adopt a resilient attitude that transforms bad luck into good."

His extensive research revealed that "luck" can be attributed more to mindset than circumstance. Much of what we interpret as good and bad luck is simply a result of our thoughts and beliefs.

That's not to say that bad things don't happen to good people

– it's just that lucky people have a way of finding the good in the bad and making the most of every opportunity.

## The Story of the Taoist Farmer

There's an old Chinese story of a farmer who had only one horse which he used to till his fields. One day, the horse escaped into the hills and the farmer's neighbors sympathized with the old man over his bad luck. They said, "I'm so sorry. This is such bad news. You must be so upset."

The farmer replied, "Bad luck? Good luck? Who knows?" A few days later, his horse came back with twenty wild horses following. The man and his son corralled all 21 horses.

This time the neighbors congratulated the farmer on his good luck. "Congratulations! This is such good news. You must be so happy!" His reply was, "Good luck? Bad luck? Who knows?"

Then, one of the wild horses kicked the man's only son, breaking both his legs. Everyone thought this very bad luck. His neighbors said, "I'm so sorry. This is such bad news. You must be so upset." Not the farmer, whose only reaction was, "Bad luck? Good luck? Who knows?"

A few weeks later, the army marched into the village and drafted every able-bodied young man to fight. When they saw the farmer's son with his broken legs, they left him behind. The war was terrible and long, every young man was killed, but the farmer's son was spared because of his broken legs.

Now was that good luck or bad luck?

Who knows?

The only constant in life is change. It's only our limited perspective that labels things good or bad. There is always something good to be found in the bad and bad in the good, if you choose to look at it that way.

I prefer to simply say, "It is what it is".

Get in the habit of cultivating your own good luck by

determining that it is stable and largely within your own control. To the degree that it's a matter of attitude and perception, you can enhance your luck with the following exercise.

Your mindset influences your perception of reality. Your experiences in the world are influenced and shaped by the attitudes in your mind. Improve your own attitude and mindset by making yourself more lucky and open yourself up to new opportunities in life. Expect the best from every situation and interaction – and you just may find it. Create your own luck instead of hoping for pennies from heaven.

# Make Your Own Luck Exercise

- Convince yourself that everything happens for a reason. It doesn't matter if that statement is empirically true or not, it's in your own best interest to believe it. Life happens for you, not to you.

- Believe that you are lucky. Allow that belief to become a self-fulfilling prophesy. You will begin to notice chance opportunities and be in the right frame of mind to act on them.

- When bad things happen, get in the habit of imagining that you are, in fact, lucky because things could have been worse. If you get a cold, you're lucky you didn't get the flu. If you get the flu, you're lucky you didn't get pneumonia. And so on. Whatever happens, you're always lucky.

- Trust your feelings, Luke. Yoda was right. Listen to your instincts. Especially when experiencing paralysis by analysis, let your gut be your guide.

- If things are not going your way, find a way to flip the script and transform events to serve as lessons or opportunities. Your mindset and perspective will determine your take-away.

# 20

# Practice Makes Permanent

Many years ago, long before I became in demand as a speaker and entertainer, I decided to learn sleight of hand magic. Now if you've never learned magic tricks before you may be surprised to discover that most are actually very simple. Once you know the secret, you've learned the trick. But that doesn't mean you can perform it. To perform it well, you need to acquire enough skill to make the technique of executing that trick invisible to the audience, and that can take years of practice.

Learning can happen in an instant. Practicing is a life long process. I spent countless hours practicing card sleights and it's given me a skill I still possess years later. Even though there's no place for a card routine in the corporate speeches and shows I do today, the discipline of focused practice has proved to be invaluable.

I have performed my psychological illusion show literally thousands of times. The exact same show. It never gets boring because I'm always excited to make incremental improvements in my presentation. That perspective keeps the passion alive so every show is fresh, dynamic, and engaging. Each show becomes an interactive practice session with the audience as my partner in the creative process. I'm sure you've heard the saying "practice makes perfect", but it's not true. The way you practice will determine your results. The secret to practicing well is to make the process of practicing the objective, not the goal for which you began practicing in the first place. Whew, that sentence is a mouthful, but it's true.

Set a worthwhile goal, then detach from it. Don't judge your progress by regretting your mistakes or anticipating your achievements. Just stay in the present moment and practice with the objective of deliberate improvement. The larger goal will guide your efforts.

Instead of becoming bored and impatient as you make your way toward your goal, you will feel the continuous satisfaction of making incremental improvements along the way. Practice is not something to get through so you can have the satisfaction of reaching your goal, practice is the most satisfying thing about having a goal in the first place. Goals change and once attained a new one is waiting to replace it, so the satisfaction of the acquisition is fleeting. I've said several times in this book that "the work is it's own reward" and this is what I mean.

We opened this final section of the book with a quote, "success is the progressive realization of a worthy goal or ideal". Notice that has nothing to do with the attainment of that goal. It has everything do do with the process of progressively realizing it. That distinction can transform your life, because life is our opportunity to practice becoming the best and highest version of ourselves.

Practice doesn't make perfect, it makes permanent. If you practice without focus then your results will be unrewarding. If you practice with focus, and have a meaningful goal toward which you are working, then the process itself can be continuously rewarding.

## How To Practice With Focus

- Set a worthwhile goal and then emotionally detach from attaining it. Just hold it in your mind.

- Practice one thing at a time that will move you toward that goal.

- Make the process of practicing the objective of your efforts – the larger goal will serve to guide the direction of that process.

- Stay in the present moment – banish judgment, anticipation, and regret.

- Observe outcomes and dispassionately adjust your efforts accordingly.

- Be deliberate about repeating this process over and over so as to improve your results in the direction of your worthwhile goal.

- Apply this process to every exercise in this book and eventually to every area of your life – how you do anything is how you do everything.

Resolve to do everything as well as you can possibly do it – whether it's working on your golf swing, plating a meal, giving a speech, or preparing a proposal. Then practice doing that with the intention of improving your results. Live in that reality and everything you do will become an exciting adventure. It will give you life long passion, focus, and peace of mind. It's what real success is all about.

# ABOUT THE AUTHOR

**Joshua Seth** is an internationally acclaimed speaker, author, psychological illusionist and voice over artist.

As a speaker and author, he's published three books on personal improvement, public speaking, and productivity. He presents at over 100 events each year for leading Universities including Harvard, Stanford, and Oxford; as well as Fortune 500 companies including Siemens, Pfizer, and Deloitte, among others.

As a psychological illusionist he's won awards from Hollywood's famed Magic Castle, starred in four of his own prime-time TV specials in Japan and South Korea, and performed at over 2,000 events in over 30 countries, making him a real life International Man of Mystery.

And as one of Hollywood's top voice actors Joshua has given life to hundreds of commercials, thousands of promos, and over 65 TV series and feature films. Audiences will recognize Joshua as the starring role of Tai on the hit TV show and Movie *Digimon*, various voices on *Spongebob Squarepants*, the announcer on *The Batman*, and the title role in the critically acclaimed anime movie *Akira*, to name a few.

Joshua Seth trained as a performing artist at New York University's Tisch School of the Arts in Manhattan where he completed a 4 year program in just 2 years, with a double major, and no caffeine. How did he do it? Focus.

He lives on the gulf coast of Florida with his wife and two children and enjoys paddle boarding, golfing, and being a dad.

Visit Joshua at www.joshuaseth.com

# Your Next Step

If you haven't done so already, get the top 5 (free) tools I use every day to increase focus and productivity. It's the best way to start putting all this information into action.

**Guided Meditation Audio:** A progressive relaxation recording that will help you melt away stress, overwhelm, and fatigue

**Daily Action Plan:** Downloadable PDF to help systemize your day

**Morning Systemization Form:** Downloadable PDF to help start the day off right

**The Email Game:** Get to Inbox Zero fast (and stay there) while having fun along the way.

**Online Resources:** Get info on all the latest websites, software, and apps to help you get to inbox zero, time your workflows, and consume content up to 5 times faster.

**For Instant Access Visit**
**www.findingfocusbook.com**

For Information On A Live Joshua Seth
Keynote Presentation or Psychological Illusion Show
at Your Company Event Visit
**www.joshuaseth.com**

42091442R00081

Made in the USA
Lexington, KY
08 June 2015